SWU-800-014

UNIFORMS OF RUSSIAN ARMY DURING THE YEARS 1825-1855 VOL. 14

UNDER THE REIGN OF NICHOLAS I
EMPEROR OF RUSSIA BETWEEN 1825 TO 1855
IRREGULAR TROOPS, FLAGS & OTHERS - PART 2

From the Viskovatov's greatest work:
"Historical description of the clothing and
arms of the Russian Army"

English translation by Mark Conrad

SOLDIERSHOP PUBLISHING

AUTHOR
Aleksandr Vasilevich Viskovatov born 22 April (4 May New Style) 1804, died 27 February (11 March) 1858 in St. Petersburg, Russian military historian. He graduated from the 1st Cadet Corps and served in the artillery, the hydrographic depot of the Naval Ministry, and then in the Department of Military Educational Institutions. He mainly studied historical artifacts and the histories of military units. Viskovatov's greatest work was the Historical Description of the Clothing and Arms of the Russian Army.

PUBLISHING'S NOTE
None of **unpublished** images or text of our book may be reproduced in any format without the expressed written permission of Soldiershop.com when not indicate as marked with license creative commons 3.0 or 4.0. The publisher remains to disposition of the possible having right for all the doubtful sources images or not identifies. Our trademark: Soldiershop Publishing @, The names of our series: Soldiers&Weapons, Battlefield, War in colour, PaperSoldiers, Soldiershop e-book etc. are herein @ by Soldiershop.com.

NOTE ABOUT BOOK PRINTING BEFORE 1925
This book may contain text or images coming from a reproduction of a book published before 1925 (over seventy years ago). No effort has been made to modernize or standardize the spelling used in the original text, so this book may have occasional imperfections such as missing or blurred pages, poor pictures, errant marks, etc. that were either part of the original artifact, or were introduced by the scanning process. We believe this work is culturally important, and despite the imperfections, have elected to bring it back into print (digital and/or paper) as part of our continuing commitment to the preservation of printed works worldwide. We appreciate your understanding of the imperfections in the preservation process, and hope you enjoy this valuable book. Now this book is purpose re-built and is proof-read and re-type set from the original to provide an outstanding experience of reflowing text, also for an ebook reader. However Soldiershop publishing added, enriched, revised and overhauled the text, images, etc. of the cover and the book. Therefore, the job is now to all intents and purposes a derivative work, and the added, new and original parts of the book are the copyright of Soldiershop. On this second unpublished part of the book none of images or text may be reproduced in any format without the expressed written permission of Soldiershop. Almost many of the images of our books and prints are taken from original first edition prints or books that are no longer in copyright and are therefore public domain. We have been a specialized bookstore for a long time so we (and several friends antiquarian booksellers) have readily available a lot of ancient, historical and illustrated books not in copyright. Each of our prints, art designs or illustrations is either our own creation, or a fully digitally restoration by our computer artists, or non copyrighted images. All of our prints are "tagged" with a registered digital copyright. Soldiershop remains to disposition of the possible having right for all the doubtful sources images or not identifies.

LICENSES COMMONS
Much of the text in this book are from the *"Memoirs of the Empress Catherine II., by Catherine II, Empress of Russia"* This book is for the use of anyone anywhere at no cost and with almost no restrictions whatsoever. You may copy it, give it away or re-use it under the terms of the similar creative commons License. This book may utilize material marked with license creative commons 3.0 or 4.0 (CC BY 4.0), (CC BY-ND 4.0), (CC BY-SA 4.0) or (CC0 1.0). We give appropriate attribution credit and indicate if change were made below in the acknowledgements field.

ACKNOWLEDGEMENTS
A Special Thanks to NYPL and other institutions for their kindly permission to use some images of his archives, collections or books used in our book.

Title: **UNIFORMS OF RUSSIAN ARMY DURING THE YEARS 1825-1855. VOL. 14** -Under the reign of Nicholas I emperor of Russia between 1825-1855
By A.V.Viskovatov. Serie edit by Luca S. Cristini. First edition by Soldiershop. July 2019
Cover & Art Design: Luca S. Cristini. Plates re-colorations by Anna Cristini. ISBN code: 978-88-93274319
Published by Luca Cristini Editore, via Orio 35/4- 24050 Zanica (BG) ITALY. www.soldiershop.com

UNIFORMS OF THE RUSSIAN ARMY DURING THE YEARS 1825-1855 VOL. 14

UNDER THE REIGN OF NICHOLAS I EMPEROUR OF RUSSIA BETWEEN 1825 AND 1855

*

IRREGULAR TROOPS, FLAGS & OTHERS - PART. 2

Portrait of two officers of irregular cossacks

HISTORICAL DESCRIPTION OF THE CLOTHING AND ARMS OF THE RUSSIAN ARMY - A.V. VISKOVATOV
(First English translation by Mark Conrad)

Soldiershop is glad to presents the complete collection of the great job made by A.V. Viskovatov dedicated to the uniforms and weapons belonging from the first Zar and Russian emperors to the Russian army during the Napoleonic period, until 1860 about. The time we considered in this volume corresponds to the reigns of Nicholas I that was the Emperor of Russia from 1825 until 1855. He was also the King of Poland and Grand Duke of Finland. He is best known as a political conservative whose reign was marked by geographical expansion, repression of dissent, economic stagnation, poor administrative policies, a corrupt bureaucracy, and frequent wars that culminated in Russia's defeat in the Crimean War of 1853–56.
Our reprint in based on the original 19th century volumes. This part is distributed at now on six volumes.
Our new edition, the first ever published in English, both on paper and digital format, boasts a large number of color plates, many of them unpublished and re-coloured by our team of expert artists and scholars of uniformology. Each volume is based on 100 color plates or more, always accompanied by the original translated text which describes the subjets of the plates.
A unique work in its genre, a must have in any respecting collection!

Aleksandr Vasilevich Viskovatov born 22 April (4 May New Style) 1804, died 27 February (11 March) 1858 in St. Petersburg, Russian military historian. He graduated from the 1st Cadet Corps and served in the artillery, the hydrographic depot of the Naval Ministry, and then in the Department of Military Educational Institutions. He mainly studied historical artifacts and the histories of military units. Viskovatov's greatest work was the Historical Description of the Clothing and Arms of the Russian Army (Vols. 1-30, St. Petersburg, 1841-62; 2nd ed. Vols. 1-34, St. Petersburg - Novosibirsk - Leningrad, 1899-1948). This work is based on a great quantity of archival documents and contains four thousand colored illustrations.

Viskovatov was the author of Chronicles of the Russian Army (Books 1-20, St. Petersburg, 1834-42) and Chronicles of the Russian Imperial Army (Parts 1-7, St. Petersburg, 1852). He collected valuable material on the history of the Russian navy which went into A Short Overview of Russian Naval Campaigns and General Voyages to the End of the XVII Century (St. Petersburg, 1864; 2nd edition Moscow, 1946). Together with A.I. Mikhailovskii-Danilevskii he helped prepare and create the Military Gallery in the Winter Palace.
He wrote the historical military inscriptions for the walls of the Hall of St. George in the Great Palace of the Kremlin. (From the article in the Soviet Military Encyclopedia.)

CONTENTS

*

Preface pag. 5

XII - Little Russian cossack regiments. Pag. 7

XII - Danube cossack Host Pag. 7

XIV - Azov cossack Host Pag. 8

XV - Life Guard Crimean tatar squadron. Pag. 10

XVI - Balakava Greek infantry battalion Pag. 12

XVII - Uniformos of temporary forces Pag. 12

XVIII - Flags and standards Pag. 14

XIX - Order ribbons and metal bands for flags and standards Pag. 33

XX - Orders and medals Pag. 34

*

Notes pag. 35

PLATES pag.39

HISTORICAL DESCRIPTION OF THE CLOTHING AND ARMS OF THE RUSSIAN ARMY
Irregular Troops, Temporary Forces, Flags, Orders, and Medals 1825-1855 part 2

Chapter XII. LITTLE-RUSSIAN COSSACK REGIMENTS. [*MARLOROSSIISKIE KAZACHIE POLKI.*]

6 May 1831 - Along with the order to form eight mounted regiments from **Little-Russian cossacks** in Chernigov and Poltava provinces under the titles of 1st, 2nd, 3rd, 4th, 5th, 6th, 7th, and 8th Little-Russian Cossack Regiments, it is ordered that each cossack in these regiments be provided from local public resources with a cloth half-caftan, one pair of cloth sharovary pants and two linen pairs of drawers, a greatcoat, black cap of sheep's fleece, black cloth neckcloth, three shirts and two pairs of boots, a flask for water, rope lasso 10 sazhens [70 feet] long, bags, a small cloth valise, nagaika whip, and a lance of forged iron.
Arms—saber with sword belt, cartridge pouch [*lyadunka*] with crossbelt, and one pistol, all being ordered to be provided by the government. The uniforms for these regiments are prescribed to be dark green with red piping on collar and cuffs, and with white appointments (Illus. 1278). Officers are ordered to have silver epaulettes with scales, with small gilt stars and the number of the regiment (Illus. 1279). Cossacks are allowed to be dressed in gray cloth at first (with the regimental number on the shoulder straps), but officers must have the established uniform immediately (163).
18 May 1838 - For the 1st and 2nd Little-Russian Cossack Regiments, remaining after the disbandment of the others, **shashkas** are established in place of sabers (Illus. 1280), and afterward the their uniform and arms did not change, for the 2nd Regiment up to 1839, and for the 1st to 1842, when they became part of the Caucasian Line Cossack Host (164).

Chapter XIII. DANUBE COSSACK HOST. [*DUNAISKOE KAZACH'E VOISKO.*]

16 March 1837, 29 April 1838 - The Danube Cossack Host is prescribed uniforms, accouterments, and weapons, as well as horse furniture, as for the Don Host, with only the red cloth used a distinction changed to **light blue** [*svetlosinii*] cloth, and red tape and cords—to **light blue** (Illus. 1281 and 1282) (165).
2 January 1844 - There is to be a metallic **cockade** on the capband of officers' forage caps, as established at this same time for officers' caps in the regular forces (166).
20 May 1844 - With the general allocation of **forage cap** colors throughout the Military Administration, in the Danube Cossack Host forage caps are to be dark blue [*sinii*], with a light-blue band and light-blue piping around the top (167).
13 December 1844 - By an administrative regulation confirmed on this date for the **Danube Cossack Host**, its uniforms, weapons, and horse equipment remain unchanged, but described in all details.
Lower ranks in regiments.
Headdress of black astrakhan with a light-blue cloth bag and chinstrap. White upper pompon, of wool, with light-blue cloth lining on the lower pompon. Black neckcloth. Jacket of dark-blue cloth with light-blue piping along the collar and cuffs. Dark-blue cloth sharovary pants with light-blue stripes. Girdle—of light-blue shalloon. Gray cloth greatcoat with a collar of the same with light-blue tabs. Boots with iron spurs. Dark-blue shoulder straps with light-blue piping and the regimental number, with a white metal button. Sword knot of black leather. Dark-blue cloth forage cap, with band and piping of light-blue cloth, without a visor.
Ammunition pouch for 40 rounds in iron pockets laid out in 2 rows, with black leather sewn around, and lid of the same leather, and stitching along the edges. The cartridge-carrier crossbelt is a black rawhide strap 3/4 vershok [1-1/4 inches] wide, with brass buckles, slides, and endpieces. Carrier for stowing the pistol—of black leather with two side flaps and stitching along the edges; 4 vershoks [7 inches] long on the left side and 5 [8-3/4] on the right; the width at the top 4 vershoks [7 inches], and at the bottom 1-3/4 [3]. Pistol lanyard of dark-blue wool, with one tassel and two slides, 2 arshins 7 vershoks [68-1/4 inches] long.
Pistol case—of dark-blue cloth to the lower part of the firelock, of shiny black leather from that part; above, where the

cloth ends, it is trimmed around with dark-blue tape; for closure around the butt there is a dark-blue wool cord with tassel; the case is 9-1/2 vershoks [16-5/8 inches] long, 3-1/2 [6-1/8] wide at the bottom and 1-3/4 [3] in the middle, the circumference of the bottom is 2-1/2 vershoks [4-3/8 inches]; tape on the cases is 1/4 vershok [1/2 inch] wide. Sword belt of shiny black leather with three brass buckles; width of the strap - 6/8 vershok [1-1/4 inches].

Saddlecloth of dark-blue army cloth with canvas lining, trimmed on the edges with light-blue cloth tape 7/8 vershok [1-1/2 inches] wide; on the rear corners of the saddlecloth is the same tape, 9-1/2 vershoks [16-5/8 inches] in length. Cushion of dark-blue army cloth with canvas lining, trimmed around the seam with light-blue cloth tape 7/8 vershok [1-1/2 inches] wide. Valise of gray army cloth with canvas lining, four white metal buttons, and the regimental number; the valise is 14-1/2 vershoks [24-1/2 inches] long, the circumference of the ends is 12-3/4 vershoks [22-1/3 inches].

Saddle with appurtenences in the usual cossack style. Bridle, crupper, and chestband—without any fittings. Sweat-cloth with cover—of fine white felt in five layers, covered on top, reinforced below with black calf-skin. Pack strap [*v'yuchnyi remen'*] of black rawhide with a brass buckle, 1 arshin 7 vershoks [40-1/4 inches] long.

Shashka sword—brass handle, bands with rings, and endpiece; wooden scabbard wrapped with black leather. Pistol of the pattern adopted by the cavalry, worn in a carrier fastened behind on the sword belt. Musket and sling according to the pattern confirmed 28 April 1838. Musket case of shaggy black felt with a sling made from a black rawhide strap 5/8 vershok [1-1/10 inches] wide. Horse cloth—of gray cloth. Lance with a black shaft (Illus. 1283).

Non-commissioned officers and clerks have white galloon on the collar and cuffs.

Officers.

Silver upper pompon on the headdress, light-blue cloth lining on the lower pompon. Dark-blue cloth jacket; silver buttonhole loops on the collar and cuffs with light-blue piping. Dark-blue cloth chekmen, with collar of the same and light-blue piping around the collar and cuffs. Light-blue silk girdle. Silver epaulettes and sash, of the confirmed pattern. Silver sword knot on a black strap. Forage cap the same as for lower ranks, but with a visor and cockade.

Ammunition pouch for 20 rounds in iron pockets laid out in one row; pockets lined with black morocco, trimmed at the bottom along the seam with thin black silk cord, and with a black morocco lid trimmed around the edge with silver lace without a light. Cartridge-carrier crossbelt of silver lace without a light, backed with black morocco 11/16 vershok [1-1/5 inches] wide, with silver buckles, slides, and endpieces. Carrier for stowing the pistol—of black morocco, with two side flaps and stitching along the sides; 1-7/8 vershoks [3-1/4 inches] long on the left side, 3-1/2 [6-1/8] on the right; 3 vershoks [5-1/4 inches] wide at the top, 1-1/2 [2-5/8] at the bottom.

Pistol lanyard—silver with one tassle and two slides, 2 arshins 10 vershoks [73-1/2 inches] long. Pistol case—of dark-blue cloth to the lower part of the firelock, from the lower part of the lock of black morocco; at the top, where the cloth ends, and below at the very end, it is trimmed around with silver lace without a light. A black silk cord for tying around the butt. The case is 7 vershoks [12-1/4] inches long, 3-3/4 [6-1/2] wide at the top, 1-3/4 [3] at the middle, and 2 [3-1/2] in circumference at the bottom; lace on the cases 3/8 vershok [2/3 inch] wide.

Sword belt—of the pattern established for light cavalry, modified so that the waistbelt is whole and to it are sewn the slings on an oval ring which is only half visible, and so that the sword belt is sewn on the waistbelt and slings with silver lace without a light.

Dark-blue cloth saddlecloth, reinforced with black calf-skin; trimmed around the edges with light-blue tape 3/4 vershok [1-1/4 inches] wide; the same tape is on the corners of the saddlecloth, 5-1/2 vershoks [9-1/2 inches] in length in the front and 9 [15-3/4] at the rear. Cushion of dark-blue cloth backed with black calf-skin; trimmed around along the seam with light-blue tape 3/4 vershok [1-1/4 inches] wide. Valise of gray cloth with leather reinforcement, four white metal buttons, and the regimental number; valise 12 vershoks [21 inches] long, the ends 9 [15-3/4 inches] around.

Shashka with gilt handle, bands with rings, and endpiece. Wooden scabbard wrapped in black morocco.

The headdress, neckcloth, sharovary, and other pieces of uniform clothing, weaponry, and horse furniture follow the patterns prescribed for lower rank except for the musket and sling and the musket case, as well as the lance, none of which are prescribed for officers (Illus. 1284). On scheduled feastdays, when they are prescribed to be in full parade or ceremonial dress, all field and company-grade officers of the Danube Cossack Host are to wear jackets. When wearing the chekmen the headdress, girdle, swordbelt, and shashka are worn; while on campaign the headdress has a cover of black lacquered leather. The adjutant to the Government Ataman is prescribed a uniform of cossack cut, of dark-green cloth with a silver aiguilette; red cloth collar with two silver buttonhole loops on the collar and cuffs; piping and girdle white; sharovary with red edging; saber of the pattern for cavalry troops. Mounted personnel on internal service.

Dark-blue cloth forage cap with light-blue band and piping. Gray cloth greatcoat with a collar of the same with light-blue tabs. Gray cloth sharovary with light-blue piping. Ammunition pouch, sword belt, and shashka—of the patterns for serving cossacks. Standard cossack pistol. Saddle of the pattern for serving cossacks, without a cloth shabrack (Illus. 1285). Dismounted personnel on internal service.

Forage cap, greatcoat, and sharovary—exactly like those for mounted personnel on internal service. Lance 2-1/4 arshins [5 feet 3 inches] long (Illus. 1286) (168).

14 April 1845 - Chekmens in the Danube Cossack Host are replaced by **jackets**, as introduced at this time in the Don, Astrakhan, Ural, and Orenburg hosts. Field and company-grade officers are ordered to wear pistols with cords only when in formation (169).

27 April 1845 - With the **changes** in uniform for the Danube Cossack Host promulgated on 14 April 1845, there are established:
Dark-blue **chekmen** as before, but reaching to 4 vershoks [7 inches] of the knee, with light-blue edging on the collar and cuffs; for non-commissioned officers their prescribed silver buttonhole loops. **Headdress** of black astrakhan, 4-1/4 vershoks [7-7/8 inches] high, without an indent on top, with a light-blue cloth bag under which is sewn an oilcloth base. Light-blue **girdle**. **Pistol case** of the previous pattern, but sewn into a holder fastened to the sword belt on the left side. All other items of uniforms and weapons not mentioned here, as well as horse furniture, remain unchanged (Illus. 1287 and 1288) (170).

Chapter XIV. AZOV COSSACK HOST. [AZOVSKOE KAZACH'E VOISKO.]

11 January 1833 - The **Azov Cossack Host** is prescribed uniforms after the style of the Black Sea Cossack Host with the following dinstinctions in colors:
Raspberry jacket, with a similarly colored collar and dark-blue sleeves, with raspberry piping along the edges of the cuffs; raspberry shoulder straps with dark-blue piping; false sleeves (on the back), raspberry with similarly colored cuffs; dark-blue chekmen with the same colored collar piped raspberry, raspberry sleeves; dark-blue shoulder straps with raspberry piping; dark-blue false sleeves, the cuffs with raspberry piping; dark-blue sharovary pants without stripes; headdress bag raspberry; upper and lower pompons, cords, and girdle—white; for officers the same uniform but with their normal distinctions (Illus. 1289 and 1290) (171).

17 December 1837 - An additional, fourth, thin twist of braid is added to officers' **epaulettes**, as in the regular forces (172).

29 April 1838 - The **changes** in uniforms for the Don Host promulgated on this day are also applied to the Azov Host, except for colors, which in the Host remain as before (Illus. 1291) (173).

8 March 1841 - The **Azov Cossack Host** is prescribed uniforms of dark-blue cloth cut as in foot battalions of the Black Sea Cossack Host, described in detail above (Vol. 29, *Historical Description of The Clothing and Arms of the Russian Army*), but with **light-blue** piping, and with light-blue tape on the cartridge-holders instead of red (Illus. 1292, 1293, and 1294) (174).

2 January 1844 - There is to be a metallic **cockade** on the front of the capband of officers' forage caps, as established at this same time for officers' caps in the regular forces (175).

20 May 1844 - With the general allocation of **forage cap** colors throughout the Military Administration, in the Azov Cossack Host forage caps are to have a dark-blue crown, dark-blue band with one line of light-blue piping around the top edge, and light-blue piping around the top of the crown (176).

14 April 1845 - Officers are ordered to wear **pistols** with cords only when in formation (177).

27 April 1845 - For the Azov Cossack Host there are established:
Dark-blue **chekmen** reaching to 4 vershoks [7 inches] of the knees, with light-blue edging on the collar and cuffs (Illus. 1295), and for officers—their prescribed silver buttonhole loops. **Pistol case** of the previous pattern, but sewn to the holder which is fastened to the sword belt at the left side.
The rest of the uniform items and weapons not mentioned here remain unchanged (178).

31 July 1851 - Officers of the Azov Cossack Host are ordered to have **everyday chekmens** and **sharovary**, after the example of Black Sea Foot Cossack battalions: dark-blue chekmens with the same colored collar piped around in light-blue and without any embroidery; collar and front opening down to the waist closed with small hooks; the cut of the chekmen in the back and on the skirts is in the Circassion style, likewise the long sleeves; sharovary of dark-blue cloth without stripes or galloon (Illus. 1296) (179).

3 January 1852 - **Jackets** replace the coat, and a coat is established of the pattern for Black Sea Foot Cossack battalions.

Officers: chekmen of dark-blue cloth cut the same as the everyday one, but shorter so that the skirts go to only 5 vershoks [8-3/4 inches] of the knees; light-blue piping and silver buttonhole loops on the collar and cuffs.

Lower ranks: the same chekmen, without buttonhole loops.

Sharovary remain unchanged. The waistbelt for officers and lower ranks, and the sword belt for lower ranks, remain unchanged. For officers, though, the **sword belt** is to be worn over the shoulder. Officers are not to wear a sash with the coat (Illus. 1297) (180).

Chapter XV. LIFE-GUARDS CRIMEAN-TATAR SQUADRON [*LEIB-GVARDII KRIMSKO-TATARSKII ESKADRON*].

15 July 1827 - The following uniforms, accouterments, and weapons are confirmed for the newly established **L.-Gds. Crimean-Tatar Squadron**:

Lower ranks.

Jacket (in summer) of scarlet cloth, with the same color collar, without cuffs, on the collar one buttonhole loop of white tape with red stripes; lace around the collar, along seams on the sleeves, and around the two pockets; with eight cartridge-holders on the breast; the holders are sewn onto red cloth (Illus. 1298). Dark-blue chekmen (in winter), with the same color collar and without cuffs, trimmed with white tape as the jacket; cartridge pockets on red cloth. Dark-blue sharovary pants with white tape along the outside seams. White girdle. White woolen epaulettes with a similar fringe. Tatar style headdress, round, red; a wide band of white tape, likewise white strips of galloon going to the center of the crown, where is set a knob or large button; black fur lining around the lower edge.

Arms and accouterments similar to those in the L.-Gds. Cossack Regiment. Lances with red shafts. Saber and cartridge pouch on a white strap. Pistol on a bandoleer, also white.

Cossack saddle. Red saddlecloth with a dark-blue pillow. Both saddlecloth and pillow trimmed with white tape.

Officers.

Officers' uniforms are similar to those of the lower ranks, but the trim is silver galloon instead of tape, with a black silk line running through, worn on the jacket, chekmen (Illus. 1299), sharovary, and headdress. Embroidered silver buttonhole loops on the collar. Silver epaulettes. Cartridge pouch on a silver belt. Sabers and sashes—as for cossack officers. Saddlecloth—the same colors as for lower ranks but trimmed with silver galloon, cord, and fringe (Illus. 1300) (181).

2 September 1827 - There are the following changes in uniforms for the **L.-Gds. Crimean-Tatar Squadron**:

Lower ranks.

Uniforms for lower ranks are as before, but all white tape and galloon on the headdress, jacket, chekmen, and sharovary is to be yellow Guards tape with a red stripe [*reika*] (Illus. 1301). Orange woolen epaulettes, with a fringe, as in the L.-Gds. Cossack Regiment. Sword belts and sword knots of red Russian leather. Round plates with a St. Andrew's star on the cartridge pouches. Red saddlecloth, trimmed with white tape, as in the L.-Gds. Cossack Regiment (Illus. 1301).

Officers.

For officers the cartridge pouch and saber are in all respects the same as in the L.-Gds. Cossack Regiment. One embroidered silver buttonhole loop on each side of the collar on both jacket and chekmen. All galloon is silver, but wider than before and of the new pattern (Illus. 1302) (182).

23 September 1830 - Officers and lower ranks are ordered to wear scaled **epaulettes**, of the pattern for epaulettes in the L.-Gds. Cossack Regiment (Illus. 1303) (183).

31 August 1832 - A new pattern **headdress** is confirmed, the same as before but without the knob (on top of the crown) for lower ranks (184).

4 July 1837 - Field and company-grade officers in the L.-Gds. Crimean-Tatar Squadron are allowed to wear in those situations where in regular forces **frock coats** may be worn—and apart from the coat with buttonhole loops—a **chekmen** without embroidery, dark blue, without any piping, as established for the L.-Gds. Cossack Regiment on 28 October 1836 (185).

15 July 1837 - Officers are given new pattern **sashes** with narrow silver lace of three rows of light-orange and black silk, as in regular forces (186).

17 December 1837 - An additional, fourth, thin twist of braid is added to officers' **epaulettes**, as in the regular forces (187).

29 April 1838 - With the changes in uniforms and weapons for all cossack hosts as promulgated on this day, for the **L.-Gds. Crimean-Tatar Squadron** there are established:

Lower ranks.

Headdresses of the pattern confirmed on 31 August 1832 for this squadron. Iron epaulettes, without a fringe, with a backing of scarlet cloth.

Ammunition pouchs (instead of cartridge pouches) for 40 rounds, of black Russian leather, with a lid of the same and a deerskin crossbelt without any fittings. Pistols of the pattern adopted in the light cavalry. Pistol carriers or holder (instead of holsters) of shiny black leather. pistol lanyards of orange silk. The upper part of the pistol cases to the firelock is of scarlet cloth, while the lower part is of polished black leather. Sword belt of red Russian leather.

Shashaks (instead of sabers) with brass handle, bands, rings, and endpieces, in wooden scabbards wrapped with black leather (Illus. 1304).

Officers.

The same headdresses as for lower ranks but trimmed with silver lace instead of orange tape.

Ammunition pouch (instead of cartridge pouch) for 20 rounds, of scarlet morocco leather, with a lid of scarlet cloth and a crossbelt of silver lace without a light, backed with scarlet morocco.

Pistols of the pattern adopted by light-cavalry officers. Pistol carriers of scarlet morocco. Silver pistol lanyards. The upper part of pistol cases of scarlet cloth, the lower of scarlet morocco. Sword belt of silver lace without a light, lined with scarlet morocco (Illus. 1305). Shashkas instead of sabers, with gilded handle, bands, rings, and endpiece, in a wooden scabbard wrapped with black morocco.

Officers as well as lower ranks are ordered to carry pistols in a holder fastened to the back of the sword belt on the left side, but they are to have these, as well as the carrier, cord, and case, only when in full uniform.

For lower ranks the horse's load is ordered to be arranged thus: behind the saddle—valise and saddle blanket; the blanket to be stowed under the valise and together with it strapped to the saddle by three black straps with brass two-sided buckles of the current pattern; greatcoat in front of the saddle, strapped to it with three of the same kind of straps with buckles; the rolling of the greatcoat and the stowage of other items, as well as all pieces of uniforms, accouterments, and weaponry in the squadron not mentioned here, including the cover for the headdress, remain unchanged (188).

2 January 1844 - A metal **cockade** is established for the front of the band on officers' forage caps, as for officers' caps in regular forces (189).

20 May 1844 - With the general allocation of colors for **forage caps** in the Military Administration, forage caps in the L.-Gds. Crimean-Tatar Squadron are established to be dark blue with a red band and red piping around the top (190).

14 April 1845 - Summer coats or jackets in the squadron are replaced by **parade chekmens** of the same color. These are ordered to be worn only on ceremonial days and during HIGHEST reviews. Officers are ordered to wear **pistols** with cords only when in formation (191).

27 April 1845 - Consequent to the changes in uniform for the **L.-Gds. Crimean-Tatar Squadron** promulgated on 14 April 1845, there are established:

Lower ranks.

Parade coat of scarlet cloth, of the exact same cut and pattern as used before this time; winter caftan of dark-blue cloth, with the only change being that it must be at least 2 vershoks [3-1/2 inches] above the knees; the coat is trimmed with orange woolen tape with a light the same color as the cloth (Illus. 1306 and 1307). Sharovary for everyday are without tape trim. Ammunition pouch for 20 rounds in 2 rows, of black lacquered leather on a white deerskin belt.

Pistol—on an orange woolen cord, with a case of scarlet cloth; the case trimmed with orange woolen tape and sewn into a holder of shiny black leather worn on the sword belt on the left side, and not behind the back.

Officers.

The same parade coat as for lower ranks, but trimmed with silver galloon instead of orange woolen tape (Illus. 1308). Everyday coat of dark-blue cloth, with two buttonhole loops on the collar; on the cuffs one row of galloon; on each side of the breast 4 small pockets of scarlet cloth for cartridges; the pockets trimmed around with galloon exactly as on the previous winter caftans, but the back sleeves, front opening, and skirts are not trimmed with galloon; length to within 2 vershoks [3-1/2 inches] of the knees (Illus. 1309). Sharovary for the everyday coat and undress chekmen are without galloon. Pistol on a silver cord, with a case of scarlet cloth, trimmed with silver galloon and sewn into a holder of scarlet morocco worn on the sword belt on the left side, and not at the back.

Undress chekmen [*vitse-chekmen'*] and ammunition pouch for officers; sharovary for the parade coat and headdresses for both officers and lower ranks, and all items of uniforms and weaponry not mentioned here, as well as horse furniture—all remain unchanged (192).

18 January 1848 - Patterns are confirmed for officers' **cartridge pouches** in place of ammunition pouches (see H.I.M. the Heir and Tsesarevich's Ataman Regiment) (193).

15 January 1851 - It is set forth that: the **musket sling** be made of two rawhide straps with one side blackened, joined together by a brass buckle and fastened to the musket by the ends being passed through the stock; the musket case be of black Russian leather lined with gray cloth and have a rawhide strap opposite the hammer; the brass kettle be carried on the right side of the valise instead of the left, in order to avoid damaging the musket and shashka; officers are not to have holsters, and **pistols** are to be in a carrier of the present pattern; lower ranks, when going out on guard duty, are to have the musket worn over the shoulder (194).

Chapter XVI. BALAKLAVA GREEK INFANTRY BATTALION [*Balaklavskii Grecheskii pekhotnyi batal'on*].

14 April 1830 - In place of the uniforms and accouterments used in this battalion since 1797, it is ordered to have new items of the following description:
Privates.
Naval pattern shako with brass army plate, with brass buttons over the chinstrap. Cossack style jacket, dark green with red collar, cuffs, and shoulder straps. Cossack style sharovary pants, dark green with red piping. Waistbelt of lancer pattern, dark green with red. Black cloth neckcloth. Gray greatcoat with red collar and shoulder straps, and brass buttons. Dark-green forage cap with a red band (no cut-out number or letter) and red piping around the top. Black leather sword belt, pistol holster of the same, with brass fittings. Black leather cartridge pouch, on a crossbelt of the same.
The saber, pistol, and musket (of an Albanian musket pattern) remain unchanged (Illus. 1310)
Non-commissioned officers.
All as for privates but with the addition of gold galloon on the jacket's collar and cuffs (Illus. 1311).
Officers.
Uniform of the cut and colors as for privates, but with chinscales on the shako, gold infantry epaulettes on a red base, dark-green frock coat with a red collar and gold buttons; silk waistbelt, black sword belt with brass fittings; sword knot, sash, and gorget the same as for officers throughout the infantry (Illus. 1312) (195).

15 July 1837 - Officers are given new pattern **sashes** with narrow silver lace of three rows of light-orange and black silk, as in regular forces (196).

17 December 1837 - An additional, fourth, thin twist of braid is added to officers' **epaulettes**, as in the regular forces (197).

2 January 1844 - A metal cockade is established for the front of the band on officers' **forage caps**, as for officers' caps in regular forces (198).

Chapter XVII. UNIFORMS AND ARMS OF TEMPORARY FORCEs [*Obmundirovanie i vooruzhenie vremennykh voisk*].

26 November 1854 - Rules for organizing the **Imperial Family Rifle Regiment** are confirmed, including the following description of clothing and weapons (Illus. 1313 and 1314).
Officers.
Dark-green cloth Russian style headdress, square, with quilted lining, width in cross-section along the upper edge from one corner to the other 4-3/4 vershoks [8-1/3 inches], height from the corner to the brim 2 vershoks [3-1/2 inches]; brim of black astrakhan 1-1/4 vershoks [2-3/16 inches] high. In front of the headdress, on the brim opposite the corner, is sewn a brass cross of the confirmed pattern.
Dark-green cloth half-caftan in the Russian style, without a collar, open at the neck in front just a little; pleats in back; fastened from right to left with 6 round gilt buttons, 6 small loops made from thin gold cord sewn to the right side. On both sides of the half-caftan are sewn cloth flaps for pockets. Piped with red cloth everywhere along the edges except the skirt hem. Alongside the piping on the front opening down to the waist are sewn two rows of gold army galloon, the first row next to the opening being narrow, 1/4 vershok [1/2 inch] wide, and the second wider, 1/2 veshok [7/8 inch]; the same galloon is used to trim the lower edge of the sleeves, which do not have cuffs. Dark-green stamin is used for lining. The half-caftan reaches to 5 vershoks [8-3/4 inches] of the knees. Dark-green cloth sharovary pants, inside boots. Epaulettes of gold twisted braid with a woven gold field, with army rank distinctions. Sash (with the parade dress instead of a girdle) and sword knot on the shashka—as for army infantry.
Standard officer's greatcoat, with a gray collar with dark-green tabs as for cossacks; officers have smooth yellow buttons, while the auditor and medical officials have white. In wartime officers and classed officials wear campaign greatcoats of the pattern confirmed for the rifle regiment's lower ranks. Girdle of red wool for girding the half-caftan and the greatcoat. Waistbelt according to pattern. White suede gloves.

Boots with long shafts with a red leather edgd. For field-grade officers, adjutants, the paymaster, quartermaster, doctor, and auditor—with spurs. Dark-green forage cap of the pattern for army jäger regiments, with a cockade, worn on all those occasions when officers in regular forces are allowed to wear the cap. Shashka—dragoon pattern. Sword belt of dragoon pattern, over the shoulder, lined with gold galloon on black leather. Knapsack with straps according to the pattern for army jäger regiments.

The auditor and medical officials are prescribed the same uniform but without epaulettes, with silver appointments. Additionally, medical officials were given shoulder straps by an order of the Minister of War dated 11 October 1854.

Lower ranks.

Headdress as for officers, with a canvas lining, quilted, weighing from 60 to 65 zolotniks [9 to 10 ounces]. Half-caftan of dark-green cloth, in the Russian national style, without a collar; open in front at the neck just a little; pleated in back; closed from right to left with 6 round brass buttons and 6 small loops made from thin black woolen cord, sewn to the right side. Piped with red cloth along all the edges except the skirt hem; sleeves without cuffs. Red cloth shoulder straps on both shoulders, with smooth brass buttons, one on each strap; the length of the strap is determined by the shoulder, its width is 1-1/2 vershoks [2-5/8 inches]; lined in the same color as the uniform. On both sides of the half-caftan are sewn cloth flaps 5 vershoks [8-3/4 inches] long, 1 vershok [1-3/4 inches] wide at the bottom, and 1/2 vershok [7/8 inch] at the top. Lining in the sleeves and the back is linen, and on the skirts of black kersey. On the inside along the waist is sewn plain tape to reinforce the pleats on the half-caftan. It is no closer than 5 vershoks [8-3/4 inches] of the knees as measured when kneeling. For non-commissioned officers the half-caftan has gold army galloon sewn around the upper edge around the neck (set back a small distance from the piping—1/4 vershok [1/2 inch]), and around the sleeves along the edges, again a small distance from the piping. On hornists' half-caftans are sewn red cloth wings trimmed with white tape after the manner of army troops.

Dark-green cloth sharovary pants, with pleats in front and behind, two on each side, with a cloth waistbelt 2 vershoks [3-1/2 inches] wide in front and 1-1/2 [2-5/8 inches] behind. On the belt are sewn two metal buttons for securing the linen lining. The sharovary reach to the ankle, and are 5-1/2 vershoks [9-1/2 inches] wide at the bottom; the sharovary are tucked into the boots.

Gray cloth greatcoat, in the style of a peasant's coat, or *armyak*, with a turned-down collar around the neck of the same cloth, 1-1/2 vershoks [2-5/8 inches] wide at the back. Closed from right to left on the side with 2 small iron hooks. Inside the greatcoat is sewn plain tape with 12 loops (of the same tape) for cinching the greatcoat in accordance with the wearer's waist size. No cuffs on the sleeves. Linen is used to line the sleeves, back, and under the skirts (8 vershoks [14 inches] long. Shoulder straps of red cloth with smooth brass buttons; the length of the strap is determined by the shoulder; 1-1/2 vershoks [2-5/8 inches] wide, backed with the same color as the greatcoat.

Red girdle of plain wool, 3 arshins 6 vershoks [7 feet 7-1/2 inches] long, 5-1/2 vershoks [9-1/2 inches] wide; when worn, the edges on both sides are folded up for 4 vershoks [7 inches] so that the girdle comes out to be 1-1/2 vershoks [2-1/2 inches] wide. The girdle is bound around the half-caftan or greatcoat directly at the waist and tied in front with a knot, with the ends tucked back up under it. Waistbelt of polished black leather with an iron buckle, 1 arshin 12 vershoks [49 inches] long, 3/4 vershoks [1-1/4 inches] wide, worn under the girdle. Shirt of normal shirt linen with a side collar. Bib [*nagrudnik*] of plain coarse cloth [*pestryad'*].

Gloves for supply train personnel according to pattern.

Mittens of dark-green cloth, army pattern; to the upper edge is sewn a cloth loop and if the mittens are not being worn on the hands, then they are passed through the loop under the girdle on the left side.

Boots of black Russian leather, welted, with an elongated forepart, the front reaching to the knee, with a small notch behind. On the shafts small folds; inside their upper part lined with red sheep leather so that a red edge appears at the top of the shaft. The shafts must be ample enough for the sharovary to be tucked inside them. Heels 1/4 vershok [1/2 inch] high. Train personnel are prescribed spurs.

Rifle [*shtutser*]. A normal ax; the handle painted black; worn in a case on the waistbelt along with a bayonet scabbard, on the left side. Rifle sling of polished black leather, of the pattern for rifle battalions, with brass buckles and a button. Cover on the firing pin of pattern adopted in the forces. Ammunition pouch of black calf-skin leather with a lid of the same, lined with canvas, with places for 60 rounds, with two iron buckles. Cartridge-carrier belt of shiny black leather, 3 arshins [7 feet] long and 3/4 vershoks [1-1/4 inches] wide. Small pouch for firing capsules, carried under the cartridge-carrier lid on the left side.

Case for the ax, of polished black leather sized for the ax blade, with a strap, closed by three leather straps sewn onto the top part that fasten to matching buttons. The frog for carrying the ax is of polished black leather with a pocket into which fits the bayonet scabbard.

Knapsack of the pattern for troops in the Separate Caucasus Corps, of black Russian leather, with a canvas lining, 12-7/8 vershoks [22-1/2 inches] long and 10-1/2 [18-3/8 inches] wide; rawhide strap for closing the top of the knapsack, 1/8 vershok [1/4 inch] wide and 1-3/6 arshins [42 inches] long. Knapsack straps of the pattern for army jägers.

Greatcoat case—standard, of raven' duck oilcloth; 15 vershoks [26-1/4 inches] long and 9 [15-3/4] wide, with three ties of black tape, each 5 vershoks [8-3/4 inches] long. Standard greatcoat straps of shiny black leather, with an iron buckle.

Kettle—according to pattern, copper, the inside tinned, with an iron handle; secured to the knapsack by a strap passed through a brass D-ring and the iron handle. The kettle with lid is 4-1/8 vershoks [7-1/4 inches] high and 2-1/4 [4] wide; the side at the lid is 7/8 vershok [1-1/2 inches]; the weight of the kettle is from 2 funts 50 zolotniks to 2 funts 60 zolotniks [2 pounds 4 ounces to 2 pounds 5-1/2 ounces].

Signal bugle as for other troops.

All noncombatant lower ranks have a uniform like that for combatant personnel, except orderlies, who do not have shoulder straps, piping, or a cross on the headdress (199).

29 January 1855 - Regulations are confirmed for the **Government Mobile Mass Levy**, including a description of the uniform and weapons for its members [*ratniki*].

Forage cap of gray peasant cloth with a visor; on it a cross cut from yellow brass. *Armyak* coat with shoulder straps 1-1/2 vershoks [2-5/8 inches] wide, likewise of gray peasant cloth, lined with linen, reaching to 1 vershok [1-3/4 inches] of the knees, cut rather loose so that a short sheepskin coat may be worn under it. Non-commissioned officers [*uryadniki*] have gold galloon the collar. Sharovary pants of gray peasant cloth, worn inside the boots. Long Russian boots. Shirt of normal peasant linen. Leather girdle, made from a rawhide strap, 1-1/2 vershoks [2-5/8 inches] wide, with an iron buckle.

Leather peasants' mittens with inserts, or of gray peasant cloth with a linen lining. Which kind of mitten each *druzhina* [battalion] is to have, leather or cloth, is left to the decision of the local noble assembly, taking into account the convenience of obtaining one or the other.

Short sheepskin coat.

Ax—for all non-commissioned officers on the official establishment, drummers, hornists, and 860 combatant *ratniki* in each druzhina. In the druzhinas of Vitebsk and Mobilev provinces for 306 *ratniki*.

Infantry musket with bayonet. If *ratniki* have their own rifles or muskets, then they are allowed to keep them in the mass levy. Spades—for 60 combatants in each druzhina, but in Vitebsk and Mogilev provinces—for 64. Leather knapsack with straps, small hooks, and rings—of the pattern used in the Caucasus. Ammunition pouch [*patrontash*]—the cavalry pattern. Water flasks—for personnel in the 1st and 3rd ranks. Kettles for personnel in the 2nd rank.

Ratniki do not shave their beards. Hair will remain cut as it was when they were in the peasantry. Lower rank cadre personnel are from internal guard battalions and invalid commands, and are assigned to a druzhina for their formation and training. They wear the same uniform as the *ratniki* and wear moustaches, but are not permitted beards. Officers of the druzhiny have uniforms of the same pattern as the men, of gray factory cloth; red girdle; gold epaulettes with cloth of the color prescribed for the division to which the druzhina is assigned (Illus. 1315 and 1316). Adjutants to commanders of provincial mass levies are prescribed silver epaulettes and aiguilette. Officers do not have beards but wear moustaches; they may cut they hair as the men.

Officers' arms consist of the standard infantry half-saber with sword knot, on a lacquered black sword belt, as for naval officers.

Actual state councilors and privy councilors, upon joining the mass levy, and if they command a druzhina, wear the uniform prescribed for the druzhina's officers, with gold general-officers' epaulettes with cloth and small rank stars, but to dinstinguish them from army generals their shoulder straps are silver.

Brigade and division commanders wear the standard army uniform, also with silver shoulder straps (200).

Chapter XVIII. FLAGS AND STANDARDS [ZNAMENA I SHTANDARTY].

(In this section regiments and other units are shown under those titles and numbers they had when they received their flags and standards.)

ARMY INFANTRY.

All flags newly granted to grenadier and infantry regiments after 19 November 1825 kept the same colors, dimensions, and patterns that they had during the last years of the preceding reign, except for the change in the corners from the monogram of Emperor Alexander I to that of Emperor Nicholas Pavlovich. Thus, for all these regiments the cross remained green. Corners for regiments of the 1st Grenadier Division were red with white stripes; in the 2nd Division—red with black; in the 3rd—red with yellow; in infantry regiments of the Separate Lithuanian Corps—raspberry with white; and in all other infantry regiments—white. Carabinier and jäger regiments (except in the Guards) did not have flags under Emperor Alexander I. Flag poles up to 1833 were as in the preceding reign: in a division's first regiment—straw colored; in the second—black; in the third—white; and in the fourth—coffee colored. If flags were granted to carabinier and jäger regiments (fifth and sixth in divisions), the poles were prescribed one general color—black.

The Lutsk and Samogitia Grenadier Regiments and the Nesvizh Carabinier Regiment, all three being in the reserve corps of forces under the command of the Tsesarevich and Grand Duke Constantine Pavlovich, and all regiments of the Separate Lithuanian Corps, had on their flags, on eagle's breast shield, the Lithuanian coat-of-arms instead of the Moscow coat-of-arms, i.e. instead of an image of St. George—an image of a galloping horseman with a drawn saber. This was mentioned in a HIGHEST Order of 9 May 1831 for the reserve and Lithuanian corps that removed all their existing exceptions from the general regulations for uniforms and the construction of flags and standards in the rest of the Russian army.

From 1827 flags were granted to carabinier and jäger regiments. For carabiniers this was the same flag as for grenadier regiments with the addition of yellow stripes between the cross and corners (Illus. 1317). For the first jäger regiments in brigades the flag was the same as for infantry with the addition of sky-blue stripes between the cross and corners (Illus. 1318a, 1318b); for the second jäger regiments—as infantry with the addition of red stripes between the cross and corners (Illus. 1318c, 1318d). Such flags were granted to the following units up to the reorganization of army infantry in 1833-1834, i.e. when all grenadier, carabinier, infantry, and jäger regiments consisted of two active battalions and one reserve battalion:

1. In the 1st Grenadier Division (green cross, corners red with white):
Emperor of Austria's Grenadier Regiment, Reserve Battalion - 6 December 1827.
King of Prussia's Grenadier Regiment, Reserve Battalion - 22 August 1826.
Crown Prince of Prussia's Grenadier Regiment, Reserve Battalion - 6 December 1826.
Graf Arakcheev's Grenadier Regiment, Reserve Battalion - 6 August 1826.

2. In the 2nd Grenadier Division (green cross, corners red with black):
Kiev Grenadier Regiment, Reserve Battalion - 3 January 1831.
Prince Eugene of Württemberg's Grenadier Regiment (Taurica), 1st and 2nd Battalions (St.-George flags with the inscription *"For taking a flag in battle against the French in Holland at Bergen in 1799"*) - 13 June 1827, and the Reserve Battalion (plain, without inscription) - 22 August 1831.
Yekaterinoslav Grenadier Regiment, Reserve Battalion - 22 August 1831.
Prince Paul of Mecklenburg's Grenadier Regiment (Moscow), Reserve Battalion - 3 January 1832.

3. In the 3rd Grenadier Division (green cross, corners red with yellow):
Generalissimus Prince Suvorov's Grenadier Regiment (St.-George flag with the inscription *"For distinction at the taking of Bazardzhik by storm 22 May 1810 and of Ostrolenko 14 May 1831"*) - 25 June 1831.
Astrakhan Grenadier Regiment, 1st, 2nd, and Reserve Battalions (St.-George flag with the inscription *"For distinction at the taking of Ostrolenko by storm 14 May 1831"*) - 25 June 1831.

4. In the 1st Grenadier Division (green cross, corners red with white, yellow stripes between the cross and corners) (Illus. 1317a):
1st Carabinier Regiment, 1st and 2nd Battalions - 23 April 1827, Reserve Battalion - 8 December 1829, and all three battalions (St.-George flags with the inscription *"For distinction at the taking of Warsaw by storm 25 and 26 August 1831"*) - 6 December 1831.
Field Marshal Prince Barclay de Tolly's Carabinier Regiment, 1st and 2nd Battalions - 23 April 1827, and Reserve Battalion - 8 December 1829.

5. In the 2nd Grenadier Division (green cross, corners red with black, yellow stripes between the cross and corners) (Illus. 1317b):
3rd Carabinier Regiment, 1st and 2nd Battalions - 25 February 1827.
4th Carabinier Regiment, 1st and 2nd Battalions - 25 February 1827.

6. In the 3rd Grenadier Division (green cross, corners red with yellow, yellow stripes between the cross and corners) (Illus. 1317c):
5th Carabinier Regiment, 1st and 2nd Battalions - 23 May 1828, and Reserve Battalion - 28 January 1830.
6th Carabinier Regiment, 1st and 2nd Battalions - 23 May 1828, and Reserve Battalion - 28 January 1830.

7. In the reserve corps of forces under the command of H.I.H. the Tsesarevich and Grand Duke Constantine Pavlovich (green cross, corners raspberry, yellow stripes between the cross and corners):

Nesvizh Carabinier Regiment, 1st and 2nd Battalions - 20 August 1827.

8. Marine and Infantry regiments, except those in the Separate Lithuanian Corps (green cross, white corners:

3rd Marine Regiment, 1st, 2nd, and 3rd Battalions (St.-George flags with the inscription *"For distinction at the taking of Warsaw by storm 25 and 26 August 1831"*) - 6 December 1831.

4th Marine Regiment, 1st, 2nd, and 3rd Battalions (St.-George flags with the inscription *"For distinction at the taking of Warsaw by storm 25 and 26 August 1831"*) - 6 December 1831.

Archangel Infantry Regiment, 1st, 2nd, and 3rd Battalions (St.-George flags with the inscription *"For taking a French flag in the Alps"*) - 7 January 1828.

Vologda Infantry Regiment, 1st and 2nd Battalions (St.-George flags with the inscription *"For distinction at the taking of Warsaw by storm 25 and 26 August 1831"*) - 6 December 1831.

Neva Regiment, 1st, 2nd, and 3rd Battalions (St.-George flags with the inscription *"For distinction at Kulevche 30 May 1829"*) - 6 April 1830.

Sofiya Regiment, 1st, 2nd, and 3rd Battalions (St.-George flags with the inscription *"For distinction at Kulevche 30 May 1829"*) - 6 April 1830.

Kopore Regiment, 1st, 2nd, and 3rd Battalions (St.-George flags with the inscription *"For distinction at Kulevche 30 May 1829"*) - 6 April 1830.

Aleksopol Regiment, 1st, 2nd, and 3rd Battalions (St.-George flags with the inscription *"For distinction at the taking of Warsaw by storm 25 and 26 August 1831"*) - 6 December 1831.

Kremenchug Regiment, 1st, 2nd, and 3rd Battalions (St.-George flags with the inscription *"For distinction at the taking of Warsaw by storm 25 and 26 August 1831"*) - 6 December 1831.

Polotsk Regiment, 1st, 2nd, and 3rd Battalions (St.-George flags with the inscription *"For the defense of Pravody against a Turkish army in 1829"*) - 6 April 1830.

Kozlov Regiment, 1st and 2nd Battalions (St.-George flags with the inscription *"For the defense of Bayazet fortress 20 and 21 June 1829"*) - 22 August 1830.

Nasheburg Regiment, 1st and 2nd Battalions (St.-George flags with the inscription *"For the defense of Bayazet fortress 20 and 21 June 1829"*) - 22 August 1830.

9. First Jäger regiments in brigades, except those in the Separate Lithuanian Corps (green cross, white corners, sky-blue stripes between cross and corners) (Illus. 1318a):

1st Jäger Regiment, 1st, 2nd, and 3rd Battalions - 25 November 1827.

3rd Jäger Regiment, 1st, 2nd, and 3rd Battalions - 2 December 1827.

5th Jäger Regiment, 1st and 2nd Battalions (St.-George flags with the inscription *"For distinction in the pacification of Poland in 1831"*) - 6 December 1831.

7th Jäger Regiment, 1st, 2nd, and 3rd Battalions - 6 December 1827.

9th Jäger Regiment, 1st, 2nd, and 3rd Battalions - 28 February 1828.

11th Jäger Regiment, 1st, 2nd, and 3rd Battalions (St.-George flags with the inscription *"For distinction at Kulevche 30 May 1829"*) - 6 April 1830.

13th Jäger Regiment, 1st, 2nd, and 3rd Battalions (St.-George flags with the inscription *"For distinction at the siege and taking of Anapa and Varna 1828"*) - 29 September 1828.

17th Jäger Regiment, 1st and 2nd Battalions (plain flags with the inscription *"For the crossing of the Danube 17 May 1828"*) - 27 June 1828.

19th Jäger Regiment, 1st, 2nd, and 3rd Battalions (St.-George flags with the inscription *"For the defense of Pravody against a Turkish army in 1829"*) - 6 April 1830.

31st Jäger Regiment, 1st, 2nd, and 3rd Battalions - 22 November 1831.

37th Jäger Regiment, 1st, 2nd, and 3rd Battalions (St.-George flags with the inscription *"For the defense of Pravody against a Turkish army in 1829"*) - 6 April 1830.

10. First Jäger regiments in brigades in the Separate Lithuanian Corps (green cross, corners white with raspberry, sky-blue stripes between cross and corners) (Illus. 1318b):

47th Jäger Regiment, 1st, 2nd, and 3rd Battalions - 24 September 1827.

49th Jäger Regiment, 1st, 2nd, and 3rd Battalions - 24 September 1827.

11. Second Jäger regiments in brigades, except those in the Separate Lithuanian Corps (green cross, white corners, red stripes between cross and corners) (Illus. 1318c):

2nd Jäger Regiment, 1st, 2nd, and 3rd Battalions - 25 November 1827.
4th Jäger Regiment, 1st, 2nd, and 3rd Battalions - 2 December 1827.
6th Jäger Regiment, 1st, 2nd, and 3rd Battalions - 25 December 1827.
8th Jäger Regiment, 1st, 2nd, and 3rd Battalions - 6 December 1827.
10th Jäger Regiment, 1st, 2nd, and 3rd Battalions - 18 June 1827.
12th Jäger Regiment, 1st, 2nd, and 3rd Battalions (St.-George flags with the inscription *"For distinction at Kulevche 30 May 1829"*) - 6 April 1830.
14th Jäger Regiment, 1st and 2nd Battalions (St.-George flags with the inscription *"For distinction at the siege and taking of Anapa and Varna 1828"*) - 29 September 1828.
20th Jäger Regiment, 1st, 2nd, and 3rd Battalions (St.-George flags with the inscription *"For the defense of Pravody against a Turkish army in 1829"*) - 6 April 1830.
32nd Jäger Regiment, 1st, 2nd, and 3rd Battalions - 22 November 1831.
42nd Jäger Regiment, 1st and 3rd Battalions (plain flags with the inscription *"For the defense of the fortress of Shusha against a Persian army in 1826"*) - 27 June 1828.

12. Second Jäger regiments in brigades in the Separate Lithuanian Corps (green cross, corners white with raspberry, red stripes between cross and corners) (Illus. 1318d):

48th Jäger Regiment, 1st, 2nd, and 3rd Battalions - 24 September 1827.
50th Jäger Regiment, 1st, 2nd, and 3rd Battalions - 24 September 1827.

After the reorganization of army infantry in 1833 and 1834 with the establishment of indefinite leave, the grenadier and carabinier regiments of the Grenadier Corps consisted of three active battalions (1st, 2nd, and 3rd), one reserve (4th), and one replacement (5th), and the grenadier (Georgia) and carabinier (Erivan) regiments of the Caucasus Corps—of four active battalions (1st, 2nd, 3rd, and 4th) and one reserve (5th); all infantry and jäger regiments of the 1st, 2nd, 3rd, 4th, 5th, and 6th Infantry Corps—of four active battalions (1st, 2nd, 3rd, and 4th), one reserve (5th), and one replacement (6th); all infantry and jäger regiments of the Caucasus Corps—of four active battalions (1st, 2nd, 3rd, and 4th), one reserve (5th) with the regiment, and one reserve (6th) with this corps' special Reserve Division; the regiments of the 19th Infantry Division (in Finland), all disbanded in 1835—of three active battalions (1st, 2nd, and 3rd), and one reserve (4th) battalion.

New flags were presented to the following regiments:

1. Grenadiers and Carabiniers.

The Crown Prince of Prussia's Grenadier Regiment, 3rd Battalion (plain) - 26 February 1833; 2nd Battalion - Alexander ribbons, 26 June 1836.

Graf Arakcheev's Grenadier Regiment (from 1835 Prince Frederick of the Netherlands' Grenadier Regiment), 3rd Battalion (plain) - 26 February 1833; 1st and 2nd Battalions (St.-George flags with Alexander ribbons and the inscriptions around the edges *"For distinction in the defeat and expulsion of the enemy from Russian territory in 1812"* and under the eagle *"1700-1850"*) - 25 July 1850.

Samogitia Grenadier Regiment (from 1833 Archduke Franz Karl's), 3rd and 4th Battalions (St.-George flags with the inscription *"For distinction in 1807 against the French and for Warsaw 25 and 26 August 1831"*) - 26 February 1833.

Field Marshal Prince Barclay de Tolly's Carabinier Regiment, 1st, 2nd, and 3rd Battalions (St.-George flags with the inscription *"For the taking of Warsaw by storm 25 and 26 August 1831"*) - 26 February 1833.

Kiev Grenadier Regiment (from 1834 His Royal Highness the Crown Prince of Orange's Grenadier Regiment; from 1849 His Majesty the King of the Netherlands', 1st and 2nd Battalions (St.-George flags with Alexander ribbons and the inscriptions around the edges *"For the feat at Schöngraben 4 November 1805, in the battle of a 5-thousand man corps against an enemy of 30 thousand"* and under the eagle *"1700-1850"*) - 25 July 1850.

His Royal Highness Prince Eugene of Württemberg's Grenadier Regiment, 3rd Battalion - 26 February 1833.

Yekaterinoslav Grenadier Regiment (from 1840 H.I.H. the Hereditary Tsesarevich's Grenadier Regiment), 3rd Battalion - 26 February 1833.

Prince Paul of Mecklenburg's Carabinier Regiment (from 1843 Grand Duke Frederick of Mecklenburg's Carabinier Regiment), 3rd and 4th Battalions - 20 February 1833, 1st and 2nd Battalions, Alexander ribbons - 25 June 1838.

Siberia Grenadier Regiment (from 1844 H.I.H. Grand Duke Michael Pavlovich's Grenadier Regiment; from 1849 H.I.M.

Grand Duke Nicholas Nikolaevich (the Elder's) Grenadier Regiment), 3rd Battalion (plain) and 4th Battalion (St.-George flag with the inscription *"For distinction at the taking of Ostrolenko by storm 14 May 1831"*) - 26 February 1833; 1st and 2nd Battalions, with Alexander ribbons and the inscription *"1700-1850"* - 25 July 1850.

Field Marshal Graf Rumyantsev of the Trans-Danube's Grenadier Regiment, 3rd Battalion (plain) and 4th Battalion (St.-George flag with the inscription *"For distinction at the taking of Ostrolenko by storm 14 May 1831"*) - 26 February 1833; 3rd Battalion, with an Alexander ribbon - 25 July 1838.

Generalissimus Prince Suvorov's Grenadier Regiment, 3rd Battalion - 26 February 1833.

Astrakhan Carabinier Regiment (from 1845 H.I.H. Grand Duke Alexander Aleksandrovich's Carabinier Regiment), 3rd and 4th Battalions - 26 February 1833; 1st and 2nd Battalions (St.-George flags with Alexander ribbons and the inscription around the edges *"For distinction at the taking of Ostrolenko by storm 14 May 1831"* and under the eagle *"1700-1850"*) - 25 July 1850.

Georgia Grenadier Regiment (from 1848 H.I.H. Grand Duke Constantine Nikolaevich's Grenadier Regiment) 3rd and 4th Battalions - 8 April 1834; 1st and 2nd Battalions (St.-George flags with Alexander ribbons and the inscriptions around the edges *"For distinctive courage at the taking by storm of the Turkish fortress of Akhalkalaki 7-8 December 1811"* and under the eagle *"1700-1850"*), and 3rd Battalion (with an Alexander ribbon and the inscription *"1700-1850"*) - 25 July 1850.

Erivan Carabinier Regiment (from 1850 H.I.H. the Hereditary Tsesarevich's Erivan Carabinier Regiment), 1st, 2nd, and 3rd Battalions - 8 April 1834; 1st, 2nd, and 4th Battalions (with Alexander ribbons and the inscription *"1642-1842"*) - 25 June 1842.

As before, regiments in the 1st Division were prescribed flags with a green cross and corners half red and half white; in the 2nd Division a green cross, corners red with black; in the 3rd Division and Caucasus Grenadier Brigade—green cross, corners red with yellow; in Carabinier regiments of all three divisions and the Caucasus Grenadier Brigade—with the addition of yellow stripes between the cross and corners.

Since 26 February 1833 flag poles in Grenadier regiments were prescribed to be yellow for the division's first regiments, white for the second regiments, coffee-colored for the third regiments, and black in Carabinier regiments, as before.

2. Infantry regiments.
(Green cross, white corners.)

Neva Marine Regiment (from 1846 H.M. the King of Naples Ferdinand II's Infantry Regiment), 4th Battalion (St.-George flag with the inscription *"For the taking of Warsaw by storm 25 and 26 August 1831"*) - 16 June 1833; 3rd Active Battalion and 6th Reserve Battalion (plain flags) - 16 June 1833; 1st and 2nd Battalions, Alexander ribbons and metal bands - 25 June 1838.

Sofiya Marine Regiment, 3rd Battalion and 6th Reserve Battalion - 16 June 1833; 4th Active Battalion (with the inscription *"For the taking of Warsaw by storm 25 and 26 August 1831"*); 1st and 2nd Battalions, Alexander ribbons and metal bands - 25 June 1838.

Prince of Prussia's Infantry Regiment, 3rd Active Battalion and 6th Reserve Battalion - 16 June 1833; 4th Battalion (St.-George flag with the inscription *"For the taking of Warsaw by storm 25 and 26 August 1831"*) - 16 June 1833; 1st and 2nd Battalions - Alexander ribbons and metal bands - 25 June 1838.

Prince Carl of Prussia's Infantry Regiment, 3rd Active and 6th Reserve battalions - 16 June 1833; 4th Active Battalion (St.-George flag with the inscription *"For the taking of Warsaw by storm 25 and 26 August 1831"*) - 16 June 1833; 1st and 2nd Battalions - Alexander ribbons - 25 June 1838.

General-Adjutant Prince Menshikov's Infantry Regiment, 3rd, 4th, and 6th Battalions - 16 June 1833; 1st and 2nd Battalions, Alexander ribbons - 25 June 1838.

New-Ingermanland Infantry Regiment, 3rd, 4th, and 6th Battalions - 16 June 1838; 4th Battalion, Alexander ribbons - 25 June 1838.

General-Field Marshal Prince Volkonskii's Infantry Regiment, 3rd, 4th and 6th Battalions - 30 April 1833; 1st, 2nd, 3rd, and 4th Battalions (with Alexander ribbons, with the inscription *"1700-1850"*) - 25 June 1850.

Olonets Infantry Regiment, 3rd, 4th, and 6th Battalions - 30 April 1833; 3rd and 4th Battalions (with Alexander ribbons, with the inscription *"1700-1850"*) - 25 June 1850.

H.I.H. Grand Duke Vladimir Aleksandrovich's Infantry Regiment, 3rd, 4th, and 6th Battalions (St.-George flags with the inscription *"In recognition of outstanding feats performed in the 1814 battles on 17 January at Brienne-le-Chateau and on the 20th at the town of La-Rothiere"*) - 30 April 1833; 1st and 2nd Battalions (St.-George flags with Alexander ribbons, with the inscriptions around the edges *"For taking a French flag in the Alps"* and under the eagle *"1700-1850"*) - 25 June 1850.

Vologda Infantry Regiment, 3rd, 4th, and 6th Battalions - 30 April 1833; 3rd and 4th Battalions, Alexander ribbons - 25 June 1838.

Murom Infantry Regiment, 3rd, 4th, and 6th Battalions (St.-George flags with the inscription *"For the defense of Pravody against a Turkish army in 1829"*) - 30 April 1833; 1st and 2nd Battalions, Alexander ribbons - 25 June 1850.

Nizhnii-Novgorod Infantry Regiment, 1st and 2nd Battalions (with Alexander ribbons and the inscription *"1700-1850"*) - 25 June 1850.

Field Marshal the Duke of Wellington's Infantry Regiment, 3rd, 4th, and 6th Battalions - 30 April 1833; 1st and 2nd Battalions (St.-George flags with Alexander ribbons and the inscription around the edges *"For taking a French flag in the Alps"* and under the eagle *"1700-1850"*) - 25 June 1850.

Mogilev Infantry Regiment, 3rd, 4th, and 6th Battalions - 30 April 1833.

Field Marshal Graf Diebitsch of the Trans-Balkans' Infantry Regiment, 3rd, 4th, and 6th Battalions - 30 April 1833; 1st and 2nd Battalions (St.-George flags with Alexander ribbons and the inscriptions around the edges *"For distinction in the defeat and explusion of the enemy from Russian territory in 1812"* and under the eagle *"1700-1850"*) - 25 June 1850.

Poltava Infantry Regiment, 3rd, 4th, and 6th Battalions - 30 April 1833; 3rd and 4th Battalions (with Alexander ribbons and inscriptions *"1700-1850"*) - 25 June 1850.

Yelets Infantry Regiment, 3rd, 4th, and 6th Battalions - 30 April 1833; 3rd and 4th Battalions (with Alexander ribbons and inscriptions *"1700-1850"*) - 25 June 1850.

Sevsk Infantry Regiment, 3rd, 4th, and 6th Battalions - 30 April 1833.

Yekaterinburg Infantry Regiment, 3rd Battalion (with the inscription *"For distinction in 1814 against the French"*), and 6th Battalion (with the inscription *"For distinction in 1828 and 1829 in the war against the Turks"*) - 14 April 1833; 4th Battalion - 1 November 1834.

Tobolsk Infantry Regiment, 3rd Battalion (with the inscription *"For distinction against the French in 1812, 1813 and 1814"*) - 14 April 1833; 4th Battalion - 1 May 1834; 1st, 2nd, and 4th Battalions, Alexander ribbons - 25 June 1838.

Selenginsk Infantry Regiment, 3rd, 4th, and 6th Battalions - 22 June 1833; 4th Battalion - 1 May 1834; 3rd and 4th Battalions, Alexander ribbons - 26 June 1838.

Yakutsk Infantry Regiment, 3rd Battalion - 22 June 1833; 4th Battalion - 1 May 1834; 3rd and 4th Battalions, Alexander ribbons - 25 June 1838.

Azov Infantry Regiment, 3rd and 6th Battalions (St.-George flags with the inscription *"For the defense of Pravody against a Turkish army in 1829"*) - 22 June 1833; 4th Battalion - 1 May 1834; 1st, 2nd, 3rd, and 4th Battalions, Alexander ribbons - 25 June 1838; 1st and 2nd Battalions (with the inscription *"1700-1850"*), 3rd and 4th Battalions (with the inscription around the edges *"For the defense of Pravody against a Turkish army in 1829"*, and under the eagle *"1700-1850"*) - 25 June 1850.

Dnieper Infantry Regiment, 3rd Battalion (St.-George flags with the inscription *"For the defense of Pravody against a Turkish army in 1829"*) - 22 June 1833; 4th Battalion - 1 May 1834; 3rd and 4th Battalions, Alexander ribbons - 25 June 1838; 3rd Battalion (St.-George flags with the inscription around the edges *"For the defense of Pravody against a Turkish army in 1829"*, and under the eagle *"1700-1850"*), and 4th Battalion (with the inscription *"1700-1850"*) - 25 June 1850.

Brest Infantry Regiment, 3rd and 4th Battalions - 11 April 1834; 1st, 2nd, 3rd, and 4th Battalions, Alexander ribbons - 25 June 1838; 3rd Battalion - 28 February 1845; 2nd Battalion 13 August 1846; 1st, 2nd, and 4th Battalions (with the inscription *"1700-1850"*) - 25 June 1850; 1st Battalion (with the inscription *"For distinction in battle against the Turks beyond the Cholok River 4 June 1854"*); 2nd and 3rd Battalions (with the inscription *"For the defeat of the Turks 14 November 1853 at Akhaltsykh"*) - 1854.

Belostok Infantry Regiment, 3rd and 4th Battalions - 11 April 1834; 3rd (St.-George flags with Alexander ribbon and the inscription *"For distinction in the war against the Turks in 1828 and 1829"*) - 28 February 1845; 2nd Battalion - 13 August 1846; 3rd Battalion (St.-George flags with Alexander ribbon and the inscription around the edges *"For distinction in the war against the Turks 1828-1829"*, and under the eagle *"1700-1850"*) - 25 June 1850; 1st Battalion (with the inscription *"For the defeat of the Turks 14 November 1853 at Akhaltsykh"*) - 1854.

Volhynia Infantry Regiment, 3rd and 4th Battalions - 11 April 1834; 3rd and 4th Battalions, Alexander ribbons - 25 June 1838; 3rd Battalion (with the inscription *"For distinction in the battle at Bar-sur-Aube"*) - 28 February 1845; 4th Battalion (with the inscription *"For distinction in the battle at Bar-sur-Aube, 15 February 1814"*) - 11 April 1846; 2nd Battalion - 13 August 1846; 3rd Battalion (with the inscription around the edges *"For distinction in the battle at Bar-sur-Aube, 15 February 1814"*, and under the eagle *"1700-1850"*) - 25 June 1850.

Minsk Infantry Regiment, 3rd Battalion (with the inscription *"For distinction in the war against the French in 1812, 1813 and 1814"*), and 4th Battalion (plain) - 11 April 1833; 3rd Battalion - 28 February 1845; 4th Battalion - 11 April 1846; 2nd Battalion - 13 August 1846.

Modlin Infantry Regiment, 3rd and 4th Battalions - 11 April 1834; 1st, 2nd, and 4th Battalions, Alexander ribbons - 25 June 1838; 3rd Battalion - 28 February 1845; 2nd Battalion - 13 August 1846; 4th Battalion (with the inscription *"1700-1850"*) - 25 June 1850.

Praga Infantry Regiment, 3rd and 4th Battalions - 11 April 1834; 1st, 2nd, and 4th Battalions, Alexander ribbons - 25 June 1838; 3rd Battalion - 28 February 1845; 1st and 3rd Battalions (with the inscription *"For the campaign to Andi in June 1845"*) - 20 March 1846; 2nd Battalion (with the inscription *"For the campaign to Andi in June 1845"*) - 13 August 1846; 1st and 2nd Battalions (St.-George flags with the inscription *"For the campaign to Andi in June 1845 and the taking by storm of the Telesh ravine in Transylvania in 1849"*), and 3rd and 4th Battalions (with the inscription *"For the taking by storm of the Telesh ravine in Transylvania in 1849"*) - 25 December 1849.

Vladimir Infantry Regiment, 3rd, 4th, and 6th Battalions - 12 May 1833; 5th Battalion - 12 December 1836; 1st, 2nd, 3rd, and 4th Battalions, Alexander ribbons - 25 June 1838; 3rd Battalion - 28 February 1845; 1st, 2nd, and 3rd Battalions (with the inscription *"1700-1850"*) - 25 June 1850.

Suzdal Infantry Regiment, 3rd, 4th, and 6th Battalions (with the inscription *"For distinction in the war against the Turks in 1828 and 1829"*) - 12 May 1833; 3rd Battalion - 28 February 1845; 1st, 2nd, 3rd, and 4th Battalions, Alexander ribbons - 25 June 1838; 3rd Battalion (with the inscription *"1700-1850"*), and 4th Battalion (with the inscription around the edges *"For distinction in the battle at Bar-sur-Aube, 15 February 1814"*, and under the eagle *"1700-1850"*) - 25 June 1850.

Moscow Infantry Regiment, 3rd, 4th, and 6th Battalions (with the inscription *"For distinction in the battle at Bar-sur-Aube"*), and 5th Battalion - 12 May 1833; 1st, 2nd, 3rd, and 4th Battalions, Alexander ribbons - 25 June 1838; 3rd Battalion - 28 February 1845; 1st, 2nd, and 3rd Battalions (with the inscription *"1700-1850"*), and 4th Battalion (with the inscription around the edges *"For distinction in the battle at Bar-sur-Aube, 15 February 1814"*, and under the eagle *"1700-1850"*) - 25 June 1850.

Butyrsk Infantry Regiment, 3rd, 4th, and 6th Battalions - 12 May 1833; 3rd Battalion - 25 February 1845.

Ryazan Infantry Regiment, 3rd, 4th, and 6th Battalions - 12 May 1833; 5th Battalion - 12 December 1836; 1st, 2nd, and 3rd Battalions, Alexander ribbons - 25 June 1838; 3rd Battalion - 28 February 1845.

Ryazhsk Infantry Regiment, 3rd, 4th, and 6th Battalions - 12 May 1833; 5th Battalion - 12 December 1836; 3rd Battalion - 28 February 1845.

From 3 June 1834 flag poles in infantry regiments were prescribed to be yellow in a division's first regiments and white in the second regiments.

3. The first Jäger regiments in brigades.
(Green cross, white corners, sky-blue stripes between the cross and corners.)

Narva Jäger Regiment, 3rd, 4th, and 6th Battalions - 16 June 1833; 1st and 2nd Battalions, Alexander ribbons - 25 June 1838.

Reval Jäger Regiment, 3rd, 4th, and 6th Battalions - 16 June 1833.

Field Marshal Prince Kutuzov of Smolensk's Jäger Regiment, 3rd and 4th Battalions (St.-George flags with the inscription *"For distinction in the pacification of Poland in 1831"*), and 6th Battalion - 16 June 1833; 1st and 2nd Battalions (with the inscription *"1700-1850"* and Alexander ribbons) - 25 June 1850.

Schlüsselburg Jäger Regiment, 6th Battalion - 30 April 1833; 1st and 2nd Battalions (St.-George flags with Alexander ribbons, with the inscription along the edges *"For taking a flag from the French at Friedland 2 June 1807"*, and under the eagle *"1700-1850"*) - 25 June 1850.

Kostroma Jäger Regiment, 3rd, 4th, and 6th Battalions - 30 April 1833; 1st and 2nd Battalions (with Alexander ribbons and the inscription *"1700-1850"*) - 25 June 1850.

Nizovsk Jäger Regiment, 1st and 2nd Battalions, Alexander ribbons - 25 June 1838.

Vitebsk Jäger Regiment, 3rd and 4th Battalions (St.-George flags with the inscription *"For distinction at the siege and taking of Anapa and Varna 1828"*), and 6th Battalion - 30 April 1833; 1st and 2nd Battalions, Alexander ribbons - 25 June 1838.

Aleksopol Jäger Regiment, 3rd, 4th, and 6th Battalions - 30 April 1833; 1st and 2nd Battalions, Alexander ribbons - 25 June 1838.

Bryansk Jäger Regiment, 3rd, 4th, and 6th Battalions (with the inscription *"For crossing the Danube 17 May 1828"*) - 30 April 1833; 1st and 2nd Battalions, Alexander ribbons - 25 June 1838.

Tomsk Jäger Regiment, 3rd Battalion - 14 April 1833; 4th Battalion - 1 May 1834; 3rd and 4th Battalions, Alexander ribbons - 25 June 1838; 1st, 2nd, 3rd, and 4th Battalions (with the inscription *"For the pacification of Transylvania in 1849"*) - 19 March 1850.

Okhotsk Jäger Regiment, 3rd Battalion - 22 June 1833; 4th Battalion - 1 May 1834.

Ukraine Jäger Regiment, 3rd Battalion - 22 June 1833; 4th Battalion - 1 May 1834.
Litovsk Jäger Regiment, 3rd and 4th Battalions - 11 April 1834; 1st, 2nd, 3rd, and 4th Battalions, Alexander ribbons - 25 June 1838; 3rd Battalion - 28 February 1845; 1st Battalion (with the inscription *"For the campaign to Andi in June and the taking of Dargo 6 July 1845"*) - 20 March 1846; 2nd Battalion (with the same inscription) - 13 August 1846; 3rd Battalion (with the inscription *"For distinction in battle against the Turks beyond the river Cholok 4 June 1854"*) - 1854.
Podolia Jäger Regiment, 4th Battalion - 11 April 1834; 1st and 3rd Battalions, Alexander ribbons - 25 June 1838; 3rd Battalion - 28 February 1845; 4th Battalion 11 April 1846; 2nd Battalion - 13 August 1846.
Lublin Jäger Regiment, 3rd and 4th Battalions - 11 April 1834; 4th Battalion, Alexander ribbons - 25 June 1838; 3rd Battalion (with the inscription *"For distinction in the war with the Turks 1828 and 1829"*) - 28 February 1845; 1st Battalion (with the inscription *"For the campaign to Andi in June and the taking of Dargo 6 July 1845"*), and 3rd Battalion (with the inscription *"For the taking of Andi 14 June and the campaign to Dargo in July 1845"*) - 20 March 1846; 2nd Battalion (with the inscription *"For the campaign to Andi in June and the taking of Dargo 6 July 1845"*) - 13 August 1846.
Uglich Jäger Regiment, 3rd, 4th, and 6th Battalions - 12 May 1833; 5th Battalion - 12 December 1836; 1st, 2nd, 3rd, and 4th Battalions, Alexander ribbons - 25 June 1838; 3rd Battalion - 28 February 1845.
Borodino Jäger Regiment (from 1839 H.I.H. the Heir and Tsesarevich's), 3rd, 4th, and 6th Battalions - 12 May 1833; 5th Battalion - 12 December 1836; 1st, 2nd, and 3rd Battalions, Alexander ribbons - 25 June 1838; 3rd Battalion - 28 February 1845.
Belev Jäger Regiment, 3rd, 4th, and 6th Battalions (with the inscription *"For distinction in the war with the Turks in 1828 and 1829"*) - 12 May 1833; 5th Battalion - 12 December 1836; 3rd Battalion - 25 February 1845.

4. The second Jäger regiments in brigades.
(Green cross, white corners, red stripes between the cross and corners.)
Kopore Jäger Regiment, 3rd, 4th, and 6th Battalions - 16 June 1833.
Estonia Jäger Regiment, 3rd, 4th, and 6th Battalions - 16 June 1833; 1st and 2nd Battalions, Alexander ribbons - 25 June 1838.
Velikie-Luki Jäger Regiment, 1st and 2nd Battalions, Alexander ribbons - 25 June 1838.
Ladoga Jäger Regiment, 6th Battalion - 30 April 1833; all battalions, Alexander ribbons and metal bands - 35 June 1838.
Galich Jäger Regiment, 1st and 2nd Battalions, Alexander ribbons - 25 June 1838.
Simbirsk Jäger Regiment, 1st and 2nd Battalions, Alexander ribbons - 25 June 1838.
Polotsk Jäger Regiment, 3rd and 4th Battalions (St.-George flags with the inscription *"For distinction in the siege and taking of Anapa and Varna 1828"*), and 6th Battalion - 30 April.
Kremenchug Jäger Regiment, 3rd, 4th, and 6th Battalions - 30 April 1833; 3rd and 4th Battalions (with Alexander ribbons and the inscription *"1642-1842"*) - 25 June 1842; 1st and 2nd (St.-George flags and Alexander ribbons with the inscription around the edges *"For the taking of Warsaw by storm 25 and 26 August 1831"*, and under the eagle *"1700-1850"*) - 25 June 1850.
General-Field Marshal the Prince of Warsaw Graf Paskevich of Erivan's Jäger Regiment, 3rd, 4th, and 6th Battalions - 30 April 1833; 1st and 2nd (with Alexander ribbons with the inscription around the edges *"1700-1850"*) - 25 June 1850.
Kolyvan Jäger Regiment, 3rd, 4th, and 6th Battalions - 14 April 1833; 4th Battalion - 1 May 1834; 1st and 2nd Battalions, Alexander ribbons - 25 June 1838; 1st, 2nd, 3rd, and 4th Battalions (with the inscription *"For the pacification of Transylvania in 1849"*) - 19 March 1850.
Kamchatka Jäger Regiment, 3rd and 6th Battalions - 22 June 1833; 4th Battalion - 1 May 1834.
Odessa Jäger Regiment, 3rd and 6th Battalions - 22 June 1833; 4th Battalion - 1 May 1834; 1st, 2nd, and 4th Battalions, Alexander ribbons - 25 June 1838.
Vilna Jäger Regiment, 3rd and 4th Battalions - 11 April 1834; 1st, 2nd, 3rd, and 4th Battalions, Alexander ribbons - 25 June 1838; 3rd Battalion - 28 February 1845; 2nd Battalion - 13 August 1846; 1st and 2nd (with the inscription *"For the defeat of the Turks 14 November 1853 at Akhaltsykh"*) - 1854.
Zhitomir Jäger Regiment, 4th Battalion - 11 April 1834; 1st and 2nd Battalions, Alexander ribbons - 25 June 1838; 3rd Battalion - 28 February 1845; 1st and 3rd Battalions (with the inscription *"For the campaign to Andi in June 1845"*), and 4th Battalion - 11 April 1846; 2nd Battalion (with the same inscription) - 13 August 1846.
Zamosc Jäger Regiment, 3rd and 4th Battalions - 11 April 1834; 1st, 2nd, and 4th Battalions, Alexander ribbons - 25 June 1838; 3rd Battalion (with the inscription *"For distinction in the war with the Turks in 1828 and 1829"*) - 28 February 1845; 2nd Battalion (with the inscription *"For the campaign to Andi in June and to Dargo in July 1845"*) - 20 March 1846; 2nd Battalion - 13 August 1846; 1st and 4th Battalions (with the inscription *"For the pacification of Transylvania in 1849"*), and 3rd Battalion (with the inscription *"For distinction in the war with the Turks in 1828 and 1829 and the pacification of Transylvania

in 1849") - 19 March 1850.

Kazan Jäger Regiment (from 1839 to 1849 H.I.H. Grand Duke Michael Pavlovich's, and from 1849 H.I.H. Grand Duke Michael Nikolaevich's), 3rd, 4th, and 6th Battalions - 12 May 1833; 1st, 2nd, 3rd, and 4th Battalions, Alexander ribbons - 25 June 1838; 3rd Battalion - 28 February 1845; 1st, 2nd, 3rd, and 4th Battalions (with the inscription *"For distinction in the war with the Turks in 1828 and 1829"*) - 20 March 1846; 2nd Battalion (with the inscription *"1700-1850"*) - 25 June 1850.

Tarutino Jäger Regiment, 3rd, 4th, and 6th Battalions - 12 May 1833; 5th Battalion - 12 December 1836; 1st, 2nd, and 3rd Battalions, Alexander ribbons - 25 June 1838; 3rd Battalion - 28 February 1845.

Tula Jäger Regiment, 3rd, 4th, and 6th Battalions (with the inscription *"For distinction in the war with the Turks in 1828 and 1829"*) - 12 May 1833; 3rd Battalion - 12 December 1836; 3rd Battalion - 28 February 1843.

Flag poles in all jäger regiments remained black, as before.

ARMY CAVALRY

All standards newly presented to army cavalry regiments after 19 November 1825, except those (until 1833) in the Lithuanian Lancer Divisin, kept the pattern and dimensions of standards received during the reign of Emperor Alexander I by L.-Gds. Dragoon, Hussar, Lancer, and Cossack regiments, but all were green, with the personal monogram of Emperor Nicholas Pavlovich in the corners and the additional difference that on standards without inscriptions for martial distinction, their place was taken by embroidery depicting laurel branches tied with ribbons (Illus. 1319a). Such standards were granted to the following units:

1. Cuirassier regiments.

Yekaterinoslav Cuirassier Regiment (from 1839 H.I.H. Grand Duchess Maria Nikolaevna's), 4th Double-Squadron (St.-George standards with the inscription *"For distinction in the defeat and expulsion of the enemy from Russian territory in 1812"*) - 3 April 1834, with silver embroidery and orange corners; Alexander ribbons for all double-squadrons - 25 June 1838.

Glukhov Cuirassier Regiment (from 1832 to 1849 H.I.H. Grand Duke Michael Pavlovich's, and from 1849 H.I.H. Grand Duchess Alexandra Iosifovna's), 4th Double-Squadron (St.-George standard with the inscription *"For distinction in the defeat and expulsion of the enemy from Russian territory in 1812"*) - 3 April 1834, with silver embroidery and dark-blue corners.

Astrakhan Cuirassier Regiment (from 1838 to 1851 Prince Wilhelm of Prussia's), 4th Double-Squadron - 3 April 1834, with silver embroidery and yellow corners.

Pskov Cuirassier Regiment (from 1842 H.I.H. the Tsarevich's), 4th Double-Squadron - 3 April 1834, with silver embroidery and rose corners; all double-squadrons, Alexander ribbons - 25 June 1838.

Military Order Cuirassier Regiment, 4th Double-Squadron - 3 April 1834, with gold embroidery and black corners; all double-squadrons, Alexander ribbons - 25 June 1838.

Starodub Cuirassier Regiment (from 1840 Prince Peter of Oldenburg's), 4th Double-Squadron (St.-George standard with the inscription *"For distinction at the taking of Bazardzhik by storm 22 May 1810"*) - 3 April 1834, with gold embroidery and dark-blue corners.

Prince Albert of Prussia's Little-Russia Cuirassier Regiment, 4th Double-Squadron (with the inscription *"For distinction in the defeat and expulsion of the enemy from Russian territory in 1812"*) - 3 April 1834, with gold embroidery and green corners.

H.I.H. Grand Duchess Elena Pavlovna's Cuirassier Regiment, 4th Double-Squadron - 3 April 1834, with gold embroidery and raspberry corners.

2. Dragoon regiments.

Moscow Dragoon Regiment (from 1837 H.I.H. the Heir and Tsesarevich's), 4th Double-Squadron - 5 April 1834; 1st, 2nd, 3rd, and 4th Double-Squadrons, Alexander ribbons - 25 June 1838; 1st, 2nd, and 3rd Double-Squadrons (with the inscription *"1700-1850"*) - 25 June 1850; with gold embroidery and red corners.

Kargopol Dragoon Regiment (from 1842 H.I.H. Grand Duke Constantine Nikolaevich's), 4th Double-Squadron (with the inscription *"For feats at Schöngraben 4 November 1805 in a battle of a 5-thousand man corps with an enemy numbering 30,000"*); 1st, 2nd, 3rd, and 4th Double-Squadrons, Alexander ribbons - 25 June 1838; with gold embroidery and white corners.

Kinburn Dragoon Regiment, 4th Double-Squadron - 5 April 1834; with gold embroidery and yellow corners.

New-Russia Dragoon Regiment, 4th Double-Squadron - 5 April 1834; with gold embroidery and dark-blue corners.

Kazan Dragoon Regiment, 3rd Double-Squadron - 27 November 1832; 4th Double-Squadron - 5 April 1834; 1st, 2nd, and 3rd Double-Squadrons, Alexander ribbons - 25 June 1838; with gold embroidery and red corners.

Riga Dragoon Regiment, 4th Double-Squadron - 5 April 1834; 1st, 2nd, and 3rd Double-Squadrons, Alexander ribbons -

25 July 1838; with gold embroidery and dark-blue corners.

Finland Dragoon Regiment, 4th Double-Squadron - 5 April 1834; with gold embroidery and yellow corners.

Tver Dragoon Regiment (from 1837 to 1849 H.I.H. Grand Duke Michael Pavlovich's, from 1849 H.I.H. Grand Duke Nicholas Nikoklaevich's), 4th Double-Squadron - 5 April 1834; with gold embroidery and yellow corners.

Nizhnii-Novgorod Dragoon Regiment, 1st, 2nd, and 3rd Double-Squadrons (St.-George standards with gold embroidery, red corners, and the inscription *"For distinction shown in the Persian War 1826, 1827 and 1828"*) - 27 June 1828; all double-squadrons, Alexander ribbons - 25 June 1838; 4th Double-Squadron (St.-George standard with the inscription *"For distinguished feats in Chechnya in 1851"*) - 25 March 1851.

3. Horse-Jäger regiments.

Pereyaslavl Horse-Jäger Regiment (21 March 1833 used to reinforce the Pavlograd Hussar Regiment, H.I.H. Grand Duke Michael Pavlovich's Hussar Regiment, and the Kazan Dragoon Regiment), 1st, 2nd, and 3rd Double-Squadrons - 7 August 1830; with silver embroidery and raspberry corners.

H.M. the King of Württemberg's Horse-Jäger Regiment (21 March 1833 used to reinforce the Mitau Hussar Regiment, Archduke Ferdinand's Hussar Regiment, and the Riga Dragoon Regiment), 1st, 2nd, and 3rd Double-Squadrons - 7 August 1830; with silver embroidery and red corners.

Arzamas Horse-Jäger Regiment (21 March 1833 used to reinforce the Yamburg Lancer Regiment, New-Russia Dragoon Regiment, and Tver Dragoon Regiment), 1st, 2nd, and 3rd Double-Squadrons - 7 August 1830; with silver embroidery and sky-blue corners.

Tiraspol Horse-Jäger Regiment (21 March 1833 used to reinforce H.I.H. Grand Duke Michael Pavlovich's Lancer Regiment—now H.I.H. Michael Nikolaevich's, the Finland Dragoon Regiment, and the Kargopol Dragoon Regiment—lager H.I.H. Grand Duke Constantine Nikolaevich's), 1st, 2nd, and 3rd Double-Squadrons - 7 August 1830; with silver embroidery and yellow corners.

Standards were designated for these four regiments but never issued. After the general reorganization of army cavalry in 1833 they became double-squadrons of various lancer, hussar, and dragoon regiments, and before that time did not have standards.

4. Lancer regiments.

Borisoglebsk Lancer Regiment, 1st, 2nd, and 3rd Double-Squadrons - 2 April 1833; with silver embroidery and orange corners.

Serpukhov Lancer Regiment, 1st, 2nd, and 3rd Double-Squadrons - 2 April 1833; with silver embroidery and sky-blue corners.

Orenburg Lancer Regiment, 1st, 2nd, and 3rd Double-Squadrons - 19 June 1828; with silver embroidery and yellow corners.

Siberia Lancer Regiment, 1st, 2nd, and 3rd Double-Squadrons - 19 June 1828; with silver embroidery and white corners.

Courland Lancer Regiment (from 1843 H.I.H. the Heir and Tsesarevich's Lancer Regiment), 4th Double-Squadron -7 April 1834; with gold embroidery and dark-blue corners.

Smolensk Lancer Regiment (from 1843 H.I.H. Grand Duke Nicholas Aleksandrovich's Lancer Regiment), 4th Double-Squadron - 8 July 1833; 1st, 2nd, and 3rd Double-Squadrons, Alexander ribbons - 25 June 1838; with gold embroidery and white corners.

Kharkov Lancer Regiment (from 1851 H.R.H. Prince Frederick of Prussia's Lancer Regiment), 4th Double-Squadron - 8 July 1833; 1st, 2nd, and 3rd Double-Squadrons (St.-George standards with Alexander ribbons and the inscriptions along the edges *"For distinction against the enemy in the battle of Katzbach 14 August 1813"* and under the eagle *"1651-1851"*) - 27 July 1851; with gold embroidery and yellow corners.

Lithuania Lancer Regiment (from 1839 H.I.H. Archduke Albert of Austria's Lancer Regiment), 4th Double-Squadron (Alexander ribbon, with the inscription *"For distinction in the war with the French"*) - 8 July 1833; with silver embroidery and yellow corners.

Volhynia Lancer Regiment (from 1847 H.I.H. Grand Duke Constantine Nikolaevich's Lancer Regiment), 4th Double-Squadron - 8 July 1833; with silver embroidery and dark-blue corners.

Voznesensk Lancer Regiment, 1st, 2nd, and 3rd Double-Squadrons - 1 January 1832; 4th Double-Squadron - 6 April 1834; with silver embroidery and yellow corners.

Olviopol Lancer Regiment, 1st, 2nd, and 3rd Double-Squadrons (with the inscription *"For distinction at the subjugation of the town of Enos in 1829"*) - 20 February 1830; 4th Double-Squadron - 6 April 1834; with silver embroidery and yellow corners.

Bug Lancer Regiment, 2nd and 3rd Double-Squadrons - 1 January 1832; 4th Double-Squadron - 6 April 1834; with silver embroidery and red corners.

Odessa Lancer Regiment (from 1845 H.H. the Duke of Nassau's Lancer Regiment), three standards - 1 January 1832; 4th Double-Squadron - 6 April 1834; 1st, 2nd, 3rd, and 4th Double-Squadrons (St.-George Standards with the inscription *"For distinguished feats in the suppression of revolt in Transylvania in 1849"*) - 24 September 1849; with silver embroidery and red corners.

Belgorod Lancer Regiment (from 1842 H.I.H. Archduke Karl-Ferdinand of Austria's Lancer Regiment), 1st, 2nd, and 3rd Double-Squadrons - 2 April 1833; 4th Double-Squadron - 3 April 1834; 1st, 2nd, and 3rd Double-Squadrons, Alexander ribbons - 25 July 1838; 4th Double-Squadron - 31 December 1851; with silver embroidery and raspberry corners.

Chuguev Lancer Regiment (from 1850 General-of-Cavalry Graf Nikitin's Lancer Regiment), 1st, 2nd, and 3rd Double-Squadrons - 2 April 1833; 4th Double-Squadron - 3 April 1834; 1st, 2nd, and 3rd Double-Squadrons, Alexander ribbons - 25 July 1838; 4th Double-Squadron - 31 December 1851; with silver embroidery and white corners.

Ukraine Lancer Regiment (from 1849 H.I.H. Archduke Leopold of Austria's Lancer Regiment), 1st, 2nd, and 3rd Double-Squadrons - 1 January 1832; 4th Double-Squadron - 3 April 1834; 4th Double-Squadron - 31 December 1851; with silver embroidery and red corners.

Novo-Archangelsk Lancer Regiment, 1st, 2nd, and 3rd Double-Squadrons - 1 January 1832; 4th Double-Squadron - 3 April 1834; 4th Double-Squadron - 31 December 1851; with silver embroidery and white corners.

Novo-Mirgorod Lancer Regiment, 1st, 2nd, and 3rd Double-Squadrons - 1 January 1832; 4th Double-Squadron - 3 April 1834; 4th Double-Squadron - 31 December 1851; with silver embroidery and yellow corners.

Yelisavetgrad Lancer Regiment (from 1851 H.I.H. Grand Duchess Catherine Mikhailovna's Lancer Regiment), 1st, 2nd, and 3rd Double-Squadrons - 1 January 1832; 4th Double-Squadron - 3 April 1834; 4th Double-Squadron - 31 December 1851; with silver embroidery and dark-blue corners.

H.I.H. Grand Duke Michael Pavlovich's Lancer Regiment (from 1849 H.I.H. Grand Duke Michael Nikolaevich's Lancer Regiment), 4th Double-Squadron - 1 June 1833; 1st, 2nd, and 3rd Double-Squadrons 25 June 1838; with gold embroidery and yellow corners.

Yamburg Lancer Regiment (from 1837 H.R.H. Prince Frederick of Württemberg's Lancer Regiment), 4th Double-Squadron - 1 July 1833; with silver embroidery and dark-blue corners.

5. Hussar regiments.

Irkutsk Hussar Regiment (21 March 1833 used to reinforce the Lubny, Ingermanland, and Aleksandriya Hussar Regiments, and the Volhynia Lancer Regiment), 1st, 2nd, and 3rd Double-Squadrons - 19 June 1828; with gold embroidery and raspberry corners.

Sumy Hussar Regiment, 4th Double-Squadron - 7 April 1834; 1st, 2nd, and 3rd Double-Squadrons (St.-George standards with Alexander ribbons and the inscription along the edges *"In recognition of distinguished feats performed in the successfully concluded campaign of 1814"*, and under the eagle *"1651 1851"*) - 27 July 1851; with gold embroidery and red corners.

Klyastitsy Hussar Regiment, 1st, 2nd, and 3rd Double-Squadrons (plain standards) and the 4th Double-Squadron (St.-George standards with an Alexander ribbon, with the inscription *"For feats at Schöngraben 4 November 1805 in a battle of a 5000-man corps with an enemy numbering 30,000"*) - 7 April 1834; 1st, 2nd, and 3rd Double-Squadrons (with Alexander ribbons and the inscription *"1651 1851"*) - 27 July 1851; with silver embroidery and dark-blue corners.

Yelisavetgrad Hussar Regiment (from 1845 H.I.H. Grand Duchess Olga Nikolaevna's Hussar Regiment), 1st, 2nd, and 3rd Double-Squadrons - 19 June 1828; 4th Double-Squadron - 8 July 1833; with gold embroidery and dark-blue corners.

Lubny Hussar Regiment (from 1838 to 1851 H. M. the King of Hannover's Hussar Regiment), four standards - 8 July 1833; 4th Double-Squadron - 8 July 1833; with silver embroidery and yellow corners.

Field Marshal Graf Wittgenstein's Mariupol Hussar Regiment (from 1843 Prince Frederick of Hesse-Kassel's Hussar Regiment), four standards - 8 July 1833; 1st, 2nd, and 3rd Double-Squadrons, Alexander ribbons - 25 June 1838; with silver embroidery and yellow corners.

The Prince of Orange's Belorussia Hussar Regiment (from 1840 to 1849 H. M. the King of the Netherlands' Hussar Regiment, from 1849 General-Field Marshal Graf Radetzky's), 1st, 2nd, and 3rd Double-Squadrons (plain standards) and 4th Double-Squadron (St.-George standard with an Alexander ribbon and the inscription *"For feats at Schöngraben 4 November 1805 in a battle of a 5000-man corps with an enemynumbering 30,000"*) - 8 July 1833; with silver embroidery and dark-blue corners.

Pavlograd Hussar Regiment (from 1838 H.I.H. the Heir and Tsesarevich's Hussar Regiment), 4th Double-Squadron - 6 April 1834; with gold embroidery and turquoise corners.

Archduke Ferdinand's Izyum Hussar Regiment (from 1851 H.R.H. Prince Frederick-Wilhelm of Prussia's Hussar Regiment), 4th Double-Squadron - 6 April 1834; 1st, 2nd, and 3rd Double-Squadrons (with Alexander ribbons and inscriptions around the edges *"For distinction in the defeat and expulsion of the enemy from Russian territory in 1812"*, and under the eagle *"1651-1851"*) - 27 July 1851; with gold embroidery and white corners.

H.R.H. Prince Frederick-Karl of Prussia's Akhtyrka Hussar Regiment (from 1845 General-Adjutant Prince Vasilchikov's Hussar Regiment), 4th Double-Squadron - 6 April 1834; 1st, 2nd, and 3rd Double-Squadrons (St.-George standards with Alexander ribbons and inscriptions around the edges *"In recognition of distinguished courage and bravery shown in the successfully concluded campaign of 1814"*, and under the eagle *"1651-1851"*) - 27 July 1851; with silver embroidery and yellow corners.

Aleksandriya Hussar Regiment (from 1845 General-Field Marshal the Prince of Warsaw Graf Paskevich of Erivan's Hussar Regiment), 1st, 2nd, and 3rd Double-Squadrons (St.-George standards with the inscription *"For distinction in the Turkish war of 1829"*) - 31 October 1831; 4th Double-Squadron - 6 April 1834; with silver embroidery and yellow corners.

Kiev Hussar Regiment (from 1839 H.I.H. Duke Maximillian of Leuchtenberg's Hussar Regiment), 4th Double-Squadron - 7 April 1834; 1st, 2nd, and 3rd Double-Squadrons, Alexander ribbons - 25 June 1838; with gold embroidery and red corners.

Ingermanland Hussar Regiment (from 1841 The Crown Prince of the Grand Duchy of Saxon-Weimar's Hussar Regiment), 4th Double-Squadron - 7 April 1834; 1st, 2nd, and 3rd Double-Squadrons, Alexander ribbons - 25 June 1838; with gold embroidery and dark-blue corners.

H.I.H. Grand Duke Michael Pavlovich's Narva Hussar Regiment (from 1849 H.I.H. Grand Duke Constantine Nikolaevich's Hussar Regiment), 4th Double-Squadron - 1 June 1833; 1st, 2nd, and 3rd Double-Squadrons, Alexander ribbons - 25 June 1838; with silver embroidery and yellow corners.

H.M. the King of Württemberg's Mitau Hussar Regiment, 4th Double-Squadron - 1 June 1833; with silver embroidery and yellow corners.

6. Lancer regiments in the Lithuanian Lancer Division.

Polish Lancer Regiment, 1st, 2nd, and 3rd Double-Squadrons - 29 October 1827; standards of the same size as before, but raspberry, with HIGHEST gold monograms, silver embroidery, fringe, cords, tassels, stripes on the poles, and spearheads; the spearhead of a different pattern from those of the standards described above; in the lower part the embroidered silver Cyrillic letters P. U. P., signifying the regiment's name (Illus. 1319b).

Tatar Lancer Regiment (21 March 1833 used to reinforce the Kargopol, Kinburn, New-Russia, and Riga Dragoon Regiments, and the Kharkov and Siberia Lancer Regiments), 1st, 2nd, and 3rd Double-Squadrons - 6 December 1827; as above, but with the Cyrillic letters T. U. P.

Lithuania Lancer Regiment, 1st, 2nd, and 3rd Double-Squadrons - 13 September 1828; as above, but with the Cyrillic letters L. U. P.

Volhynia Lancer Regiment, 1st, 2nd, and 3rd Double-Squadrons - 23 December 1827; as above, but with the Cyrillic letters V. U. P.

Up to 1831 all standards of these four regiments had the image of a Lithuanian horseman on the eagle's shield, and since that year—an image of St. George.

SAPPER AND PIONEER BATTALIONS.

With the exception of colors, all flags granted to sapper and pioneer battalions after 19 November 1825 were similar to the flags of jäger regiments and all had yellow poles. These flags were granted to the following battalions:

Instructional Sapper Battalion - 14 April 1827; sky-blue cross, yellow corners, black stripes between the cross and corners (Illus. 1320a).

Sapper Battalion, Grenadier Corps - (from 25 October 1829 the Grenadier Sapper Battalion) - 22 February 1828; green cross, corners half yellow and half red, black stripes between the cross and corners (Illus. 1320b); the same but a St.-George flag with the inscription *"For distinction at the siege and taking of Brailov and Silistria in 1828 and 1829"* - 6 April 1830.

1st Pioneer Battalion (from 25 October 1829 the 1st Sapper Battalion).

2nd Pioneer Battalion (from 25 October 1829 the 1st Reserve Sapper Battalion) and **5th Pioneer Battalion** (from 25 October 1829 the 2nd Sapper Battalion) - 22 February 1828; green cross, white corners, black stripes between the cross and corners (Illus. 1320c).

Lithuania Sapper Battalion (from 28 April 1831 the 6th Sapper Battalion, and from 20 October 1831 the 3rd Sapper Battalion) - 25 March 1828; green cross, corners half white and half raspberry, black stripes between the cross and corners (Illus. 1320d); in the eagle's shield an image of a Lithuanian horseman, replaced in 1831 by an image of St. George.

4th Sapper Battalion - 7 March 1833, the same as for the 1st, 2nd, and 5th Pioneer Battalions; 29 December 1849 - St.-George flag with the inscription *"For building a crossing over the river Teisa in the pacification of Hungary in 1849"*.

6th Pioneer Battalion (from 25 October 1829 the 5th Sapper Battalion) - 22 February 1828, the same as granted on this day to the 1st, 2nd, and 5th Pioneer Battalions; 6 April 1830 - St.-George flag with the inscription *"For distinction during the crossing of the Balkan range in 1829"*; 30 March 1846 - St.-George flag with the inscription *"For distinction during the crossing of the Balkan range in 1829, the campaign to Andi in June and the taking of Dargo 6 July 1845"*.

4th Pioneer Battalion (from 26 October 1829 the 4th Sapper Battalion, and from 20 February 1822 the 6th Sapper Battalion) - 29 September 1828; green cross, white corners, black stripes between the cross and corners; the same flag but of St.-George pattern, with the inscription *"For distinction during the siege and taking of the fortress of Varna"*.

2nd Reserve Sapper Battalion (disbanded 23 December 1841) - 7 March 1833, identical to those granted to the 1st, 2nd, and 5th Pioneer Battalions.

3rd Reserve Sapper Battalion (from 23 December 1841 the 2nd Reserve Sapper Battalion) - 6 December 1833, the same as the preceding flag.

8th Pioneer Battalion (from 25 October 1829 the Caucasus Sapper Battalion) - 13 September 1828, the same as the preceding flag, but a St.-George pattern with the inscription *"For distinction during the taking by storm of Akhaltsykh in 1828"*.

1st Horse-Pioneer Double-Squadron - 28 February 1828, a standard with silver embroidery and red corners

RIFLE BATTALIONS.

2nd, 3rd, 4th, and **5th Rifle Battalions** - 25 September 1849.

LINE BATTALIONS.

The flags granted to these battalions have a white cross and green corners, no monograms, and white poles (Illus. 1321). Such flags were granted to the following battalions.

1. **Finland Line Battalions.**

No. 1 - 3 July 1835 (from the 2nd Battalion of the former Nyslott Jäger Regiment, which had been granted on 18 March 1807).

No. 2 - 3 July 1835 (from the 3rd Battalion of the former Nyslott Jäger Regiment, which had been granted on 17 September 1833); 25 June 1850 - with the inscription under the eagle "1700-1850" and with an Alexander ribbon.

No. 4 - 3 July 1835 (from the 2nd Battalion of the former Petrovsk Infanry Regiment, which had been granted 30 September 1830).

No. 5 - 3 July 1835, with the inscription *"For distinction in the war against the French 1812, 1813 and 1814"* (from the 3rd Battalion of the Petrovsk Infantry Regiment, which had been granted 17 September 1833); 26 June 1850, with Alexander ribbons and inscriptions around the edges *"For distinction in the war against the French 1812, 1813 and 1814"*, and under the eagle "1700-1850".

No. 6 - 3 July 1835 (from the 2nd Battalion of the former Vilmanstrand Jäger Regiment, which had been granted on 16 March 1807).

No. 7 - 3 July 1835 (from the 3rd Battalion of the former Vilmanstrand Jäger Regiment, which had been granted on 17 September 1833); 25 June 1850, with an Alexander ribbon and the inscription under the eagle "1700-1850".

No. 9 - 3 July 1835 (from the 2nd Battalion of the formber Viborg Infantry Regiment, which had been granted 5 April 1798); 25 June 1850, with an Alexander ribbon and the inscription under the eagle "1700-1850".

No. 10 - 25 June 1838, with an Alexander ribbon.

No. 12 - 3 July 1835, with the inscription *"For distinction in the war against the French 1812, 1813 and 1814"* (from the 3rd Battalion of the former Viborg Infantry Regiment, which had been granted 17 September 1833); 25 June 1850, with Alexander ribbons and inscriptions around the edges *"For distinction in the war against the French 1812, 1813 and 1814"*, and under the eagle "1700-1850".

2. **Orenburg Line Battalions.**

Nos. 1, 2, 3, 4, 5, and 6 - 26 February 1835.

3. **Siberian Line Battalions.**
Nos. 1, 2, 3, 4, 5, 6, 7, 8, 9, 10, 11, 12, and 13 - 26 February 1835.
No. 14 - 1 March 1830.
No. 15 - 4 November 1835.
Nos. 1, 10, 11, 12, 13, and 15 - 25 June 1838, Alexander ribbons.

4. **Georgia Line Battalions.**
No. 1 (as Black-Sea Line Battalion No. 10) - 8 April 1834 (from the 3rd Battalion of the former Mingrelia Infantry Regiment, which had been granted on 31 March 1807).
Nos. 8 and 9 - 26 February 1835.
No. 11 (as Georgia Line Battalion No. 12) - 8 April 1834 (from the 3rd Battalion of the Crimea Infantry Regiment, which had been granted on 30 September 1803).
No. 12 (as Georgia Line Battalion 14 - 7 April 1834 (from the 3rd Battalion of the former Kozlov Infantry Regiment, which had been granted 5 December 1797).
No. 13 (as Caucaus Line Battalion 9 - 8 April 1834 (from the number received by the former Astrakhan Garrison Regiment on 1 October 1800); 25 June 1838, an Alexander ribbon.
No. 14 - 25 June 1850, with an Alexander ribbon and the inscription "*1700-1850*".
No. 16 (as Georgia Line Battalion No. 10) - 18 January 1830 and 26 February 1835.
No. 18 (as Georgia Line Battalion No. 13) - 8 April 1834 (from the 3rd Battalion of the former Sevastopol Infantry Regiment, which had been granted on 1 January 1809); 25 June 1838, an Alexander ribbon.

5. **Black-Sea Line Battalions.**
No. 1 and No. 2 - 26 February 1835.
No. 4 - 14 April 1851.
No. 5 - 8 April 1834, St.-George flags with the inscription *"For the defense of Bayazet fortress 20 and 21 June 1829"* (from the 2nd Battalion of the former Nasheburg Infantry Regiment, which had been granted on 22 August 1829); 25 June 1838, an Alexander ribbon.
No. 6 (as Black-Sea Line Battalion No. 4) - 8 April 1834, the same as the preceding (from the 1st Battalion of the former Nasheburg Infantry Regiment).
No. 8 (as Black-Sea Line Battalion No. 7) - 15 November 1841, with the inscription *"For distinction in the wars with Persia in 1826, 1827 and 1828, and with Turkey in 1828 and 1829"* (in place of St.-George trumpets obtained by the battalion from a battalion of the 44th Jäger Regiment); 25 June 1850 - with an Alexander ribbon and the inscription under the eagle "*1700-1850*".
No. 9 - 25 June 1850, with an Alexander ribbon and the inscription under the eagle "*1700-1850*".
No. 10 - 15 November 1841 (as Black-Sea Line Battalion No. 9), with the inscription *"For distinction in the wars with Persia in 1826 and 1827 and 1828 and with Turkey in 1828 and 1829"* (in place of St.-George trumpets the battalion obtained from a battalion of the 44th Jäger Regiment); 25 June 1855, with the same inscription along the edges, and under the eagle "*1700-1850*".
No. 11 (as Black-Sea Line Battalion No. 8) - 8 April 1834 (from the 2nd Battalion of the former Mingrelia Infantry Regiment, which had been granted on 31 March 1807).

6. **Caucasus line battalions.**
No. 3 (as Caucasus Line Battalion No. 7) - 8 April 1834 , St.-George flag with the inscription *"For the defense of the Bayazet fortress 20 and 21 June 1829"* (from the 3rd Battalion of the Nasheburg Infantry Regiment); 25 June 1838, an Alexander ribbon.
No. 4 (as Caucasus Line Battalion No. 5) - 19 April 1829 (from the 2nd Battalion of the former Vladikavkaz Garrison Regiment); 26 February 1835.
No. 6 (as Caucasus Line Battalion No. 3) - 8 April 1834 (from the 3rd Battalion of the Tenginsk Infantry Regiment); 25 June 1838, an Alexander ribbon.
No. 8 (as Caucasus Line Battalion No. 6) - 19 April 1829 (from the 3rd Battalion of the former Vladikavkaz Garrison Regiment); 26 February 1835.
No. 10 (as Caucasus Line Battalion No. 4) - 19 April 1829 (from the 1st Battalion of the former Vladikavkaz Garrison Regiment); 26 February 1835.
No. 13 (as Caucasus Line Battalion No. 9) - 26 February 1835.

GUARDS INFANTRY.

Up to 5 August 1830 new flags were presented with gilded spearheads, as previously, but after this date—with cast eagles of gilded or silvered bronze, according to the color of the uniform buttons. Spearhead finials were replaced by this eagles throughout the Guards infantry. After 19 November 1825, new flags were presented to the following regiments:

L.-Gds. Preobrazhenskii Regiment - 22 August 1850, St.-George flags with the inscription around the edges "*For feats performed in the battle of 17 August 1813 at Kulm*", and under the eagle "*1683-1700-1850*", in commemoration of 150 years since the designation of the regiment as Life-Guards. The flags have St.-Andrew ribbons and metal bands based on an order of 25 June 1838. (For the replacement battalion there was a flag with the same inscription but without the "*1850*" under the eagle; ; upon the disbandment of this battalion this flag was turned in to St.-Petersburg Arsenal.)

L.-Gds. Semenovskii Regiment - 22 August 1850, St.-George flags with the inscription around the edges "*For feats performed in the battle of 17 August 1813 at Kulm*", and under the eagle "*1683-1700-1850*", in commemoration of 150 years since the designation of the regiment as Life-Guards. The flags have St.-Andrew ribbons and metal bands.

L.-Gds. Izmailovskii Regiment - 11 June 1850, St.-George flags with St.-Andrew ribbons and metal bands, with the inscription "*For distinction in the defeat and expulsion of the enemy from Russian territory in 1812*", in commemoration of 50 years since the naming of the Sovereign Emperor as the regiment's honorary colonel [shef].

L.-Gds. Jäger Regiment, 2nd Battalion - 14 November 1828, St.-George flag with the inscription "*For distinction at the siege and taking of Anapa and Varna 1828*", with coloring the same as the flags of the regiment's other battalions, i.e. yellow cross, corners half green and half white, black pole (Illus. 1322a).

L.-Gds. Sapper Battalion - 29 September 1829, St.-George flag with the inscription "*For distinction at the taking of Varna 1828*", with coloring the same as for this battalion's previous plain flag, i.e. yellow cross, white corners, black stripes between the cross and corners, the pole of lacquered mountain-ash (Illus. 1322b).

L.-Gds. Moscow Regiment - 22 August 1850, St.-George flags with Alexander ribbons and the inscription along the edges "*For distinction in the defeat and expulsion of the enemy from Russian territory in 1812*", and under the eagle "*1683-1700-1850*", in commemoration of 150 years since the naming of the Preobrazhenskii Regiment as Life Guards, from part of which regiment was formed the L.-Gds. Lithuania Regiment that later came to form the L.-Gds. Moscow Regiment.

L.-Gds. Lithuania Regiment, 2nd (later 3rd) Battalion - 1 August 1832, St.-George flags with the inscription "*For distinction in the defeat and expulsion of the enemy from Russian territory in 1812*", with coloring the same as the flags of the regiment's other battalions, i.e. yellow cross, corners half red and half green, yellow pole (Illus. 1322c); 22 August 1850, all battalions were given St.-George flags with Alexander ribbons and the inscription along the edges "*For distinction in the defeat and expulsion of the enemy from Russian territory in 1812*", and under the eagle "*1683-1700-1850*", in commemoration of 150 years since the naming of the Preobrazhenskii Regiment as Life Guards, from part of which regiment was formed the L.-Gds. Lithuania Regiment.

L.-Gds. Volhynia Regiment, 2nd (later 3rd) Battalion - 1 August 1832, St.-George flags with the inscription "*For distinction in the defeat and expulsion of the enemy from Russian territory in 1812*", with coloring the same as the flags of the regiment's other battalions, i.e. yellow cross, green corners, black pole (Illus. 1322d).

L.-Gds. Finnish Rifle Battalion - 4 September 1829, yellow cross, dark-blue corners; on the eagle's breast, in a red shield, is painted in gold the coat-of-arms of the Grand Duchy of Finland, i.e. a lion with a raised sword, standing on a saber and surrounded by gold stars; black pole (Illus. 1323a).

For this same battalion, on 6 December 1833 - St. George flags with the inscription "*For distinction in the pacification of Poland in 1831*", yellow cross, sky-blue corners of which two opposite to each other have HIGHEST monograms, and the two others the coat-of-arms of the Grand Duchy of Finland as described above; black pole; the middle is as for all flags in the Russian army with an image of St. George in the eagle's shield (Illus. 1323b).

L.-Gds. Garrison Battalion - 11 July 1827, St. George flags with the inscription "*In commemoration of the feats of the Guards troops in 1812, 1813 and 1814*", white cross, corners, and poles (Illus. 1323c).

The replacement, or fourth, battalions of all twelve regiments of Guards infantry were granted new flags on 11 May 1832. These were as the flags for the other battalions. L.-Gds. Preobrazhenskii Regiment - corners half red and half white, yellow pole; L.-Gds. Semenovskii Regiment - corners light blue and white, black pole; L.-Gds. Izmailovskii Regiment - white corners, white pole; L.-Gds. Jäger Regiment - corners green and white, black pole; L.-Gds. Moscow Regiment - corners red and black, yellow pole; L.-Gds. Grenadier Regiment - corners light-blue and black, white pole; L.-Gds. Finland Regiment - corners green and black, black pole; L.-Gds. Lithuania Regiment - corners red and green, yellow pole; L.-Gds. Volhynia Regiment - green corners, black pole. All ten were St.-George flags, with eagles, and for all ten the cross was yellow. On the first two flags the inscription "*For feats performed in the battle of 17 August 1813 at Kulm*", and on the remaining eight—"*For distinction in the defeat and expulsion of the enemy from Russian territory in 1812*". Flags of the four battalions of the grenadier regiments of H.M. the Emperor of Austria and H.M. the King of Prussia (later the regiment of King Frederick-Wilhelm III) were plain for both regiments, without inscriptions, with a green cross and red and white corners. For the first of these two regiments the flag poles were black, and for the second—white.

GUARDS CAVALRY.

In the Guards cavalry, after 19 November 1825 new standards were presented to the following units (up to 5 August 1830 standards were issued with flat spearheads, as before, but after that date—with cast silvered eagles for units with that color of uniform buttons; the same eagles, gilded, replaced spearheads throughout the Guards cavalry in regiments with yellow buttons):

H.M. Cavalier Guards Regiment - 1 July 1851, St.-George standard with the inscription "*For distinction in the defeat and expulsion of the enemy from Russian territory in 1812*", in commemoration of 25 years since the Sovereign Empress was named honorary colonel of the regiment.

L.-Gds. Horse Regiment - 27 June 1851, St.-George standards with St.-Andrew ribbons for the metal bands, with the inscriptions "*For capturing several enemy flags at Austerlitz and for distinction in the defeat and expulsion of the enemy from Russian territory in 1812*", in commemoration of 50 years since the placement of the Sovereign Emperor on the rolls of the regiment.

L.-Gds. Horse-Grenadier Regiment (formerly the L.-Gds. Dragoon Regiment) - 27 June 1851, in commemoration of 200 years since the formation from Little-Russian cossacks of units that would serve as the basis of the regiment: St.-George standards with St.-Andrew ribbons and the inscriptions around the edges "*For distinction in the defeat and expulsion of the enemy from Russian territory in 1812*", and under the eagle "1651-1851".

L.-Gds. Lancer Regiment - 27 June 1851, in commemoration of 200 years since the formation from Little-Russian cossacks of units that would serve as the basis of the regiment: St.-George standards with St.-Andrew ribbons and metal bands, and the inscription around the edges "*For taking an enemy flag at Krasnoe and for distinction in the defeat and expulsion of the enemy from Russian territory in 1812* ", and under the eagle "*1651-1851*".

L.-Gds. Horse-Pioneer Squadron - 14 December 1826, white with yellow cross, with black stripes on the sides, silver embroidery and fringe, with an orange circle in the center on which is embroidered the two-headed Russian eagle usual for standards throughout the Russian army (Illus. 1324b).

L.-Gds. Horse-Jäger Regiment (later the L.-Gds. Dragoon Regiment), 1st, 2nd, and 3rd Double-Squadrons - 24 July 1827, standards similar to the one preceding, but without the yellow cross (Illus. 1324a).

H.I.H. Grand Duke Michael Pavlovich's L.-Gds. Lancer Regiment (from 1849 H.I.H. the Heir and Tsesarevich's L.-Gds. Lancer Regiment), 3rd Double-Squadron - 7 September 1832, St.-George standard with the inscription "*For distinction in the defeat and expulsion of the enemy from Russian territory in 1812*", identical, with the exception of the monograms, to the standards of the regiment's other double-squadrons, presented by Emperor Alexander I, i.e. white with silver embroidery, silver fringe, and dark-blue corners; 27 June 1851 - for all double-squadrons, in commemoration of 200 years since the formation from Little-Russian cossacks of units that would serve as the basis of the regiment: St.-George standards with St.-Andrew ribbons, with metal bands and the existing inscription, and under the eagle "*1651-1851*".

L.-Gds. Grodno Hussar Regiment, 1st and 2nd Double-Squadrons - 19 October 1827, standards identical to those granted in 1827 and 1828 to regiments in the Lithuania Lancer Division, described above, except with the change of the color raspberry to white, with the Cyrillic letters L. G. G. G. P. under the eagle, signifying the L.-Gds. Grodno Hussar Regiment. (In the 1st and 2nd Double-Squadrons of the H.I.H. the Heir and Tsesarevich's L.-Gds. Lancer Regiment (formerly H.I.H. Grand Duke Michael Pavlovich's) and of the Grodno Hussars there was, until 1831, an image of a Lithuanian horseman in the eagle's shield, replaced at this time by an image of St. George); 3rd Double-Squadron - 7 September 1832, standard of the pattern described for Army cavalry, but all white, with silver embroidery and fringe and the same letters under the eagle—L. G. G. G. P. (Illus. 1325).

MODEL REGIMENTS.

On 22 December 1836 the **Model Infantry Regiment** was granted two flags with white poles, in all respects similar to the flags of Army infantry regiments, but with a white cross and green corners instead of a green cross and white corners (Illus. 1326a).

On 17 November 1836 the **Model Cavalry Regiment** was granted a standard of the pattern described above for Army cavalry standards, but in white with green corners, and with gold embroidery and fringe (Illus. 1326b).

INSTRUCTIONAL CARABINIER REGIMENTS.
These regiments were granted flags of the pattern for infantry regiments, with black poles and a light-blue cross instead of green, and with corners of the following colors:
1st Instructional Regiment, 1st, 2nd, and 3rd Battalions - 16 January 1837, corners half red and half white (Illus. 1327c).
2nd Instructional Regiment - 11 June 1832, 1st and 2nd Battalions, corners half white and half yellow (Illus. 1327a); these same battalions - 15 January 1837, white corners (Illus. 1327b); 3rd Battalion - 9 June 1849.
3rd Instructional Regiment, 1st and 2nd Battalions - 16 January 1837, corners half white and half yellow (Illus. 1327a); 3rd Battalion - 9 June 1849.
4th Instructional Regiment, 1st and 2nd Battalions - 16 January 1837, corners half white and half green (Illus. 1327d); 3rd Battalion - 9 June 1849.

CADET CORPS.
Military educational institutions were granted flags of the pattern for Guards and Army infantry regiments, but with a red cross and variously colored corners as prescribed for each establishment. Following the example of Guards troops, up to 5 August 1830 the flags of military educational institutions had spearheads on the poles, but after that date these were replaced by eagles of gilded bronze. Flags were presented to the following educational establishments.
Imperial Military Orphans' Home (from 22 February 1829 the **Paul Cadet Corps**) - 31 December 1826, yellow corners (Illus. 1328a).
Moscow Cadet Corps (from 6 December 1837 the **1st Moscow Cadet Corps**) - 18 February 1827, corners half white and half yellow (Illus. 1328b).
1st Cadet Corps - 17 February 1832, white corners on which two of the opposite ones had an image of the Imperial monogram normally seen on flags, and on the two other corners was painted in gold the corps coat-of-arms, i.e. a crossed sword and staff of Mercury, bound with a ribbon. Under the eagle, in the lower part of the gold wreath, on a sky-blue ribbon was the gold inscription "*17 February 1732, 17 February 1832*" (Illus. 1328c).
Graf Arakcheev's Novgorod Cadet Corps - 29 October 1837, corners half green and half white (Illus. 1329a).
Polotsk Cadet Corps - on the same date, corners light blue and yellow (Illus. 1329b).
23 February 1844 - It is ordered that as a rule, each provincial cadet corps would receive its flag once the corps had its third company fully organized and armed.
9 May 1844 - It is ordered that cadet corps flags have a red cross as before, with corners of the following colors:
1st Cadet Corps - white, as before.
2nd Cadet Corps - half white and half yellow, as up to now was prescribed for the 1st Moscow Cadet Corps (Illus. 1329d). (The 2nd Cadet Corps had a flag since the reign of Emperor Alexander I.)
Paul Cadet Corps - half light blue and half yellow, as until this time was prescribed for the Polotsk Cadet Corps (Illus. 1329b).
Graf Arakcheev's Novgorod Cadet Corps - half light green and half yellow (Illus. 1329c).
Nobiliary Regiment - half dark green and half yellow.
1st Moscow Cadet Corps - half yellow and half black (Illus. 1330a).
2nd Moscow Cadet Corps - half white and half black.
Orel-Bakhtin Cadet Corps - half light blue and half black.
Michael-Voronezh Cadet Corps - half light green and half black.
Kazan Cadet Corps - half light blue and half black.
Polotsk Cadet Corps - half yellow and half dark green (Illus. 1330b).
Peter-Poltava Cadet Corps - half white and half dark green (Illus. 1330c).
Alexander-Brest Cadet Corps - half light blue and half dark green.
Tula Cadet Corps - half light green and half dark green.
Of these corps the 2nd Moscow, Kazan, and Tula were still only proposed to be established. The 1st Cadet Corps and Nobiliary Regiment kept their previous flags. In the Paul, Novgorod, 1st Moscow, and Polotsk corps the flags were changed on the basis of the HIGHEST Order of 9 May 1844. The following received new flags: 2nd Cadet Corps - 19 August 1844; Poltava Cadet Corps - 27 June 1844; Michael-Voronezh Cadet Corps - 29 October 1848.
On **25 November 1842** the following **pole colors** were prescribed for the flags of cadet corps:
1st, 1st Moscow, and Polotsk—yellow.

2nd, 2nd Moscow, and Peter-Poltava—white.
Paul, Orel-Bakhtin, and Alexander-Brest—coffee.
Graf Arakcheev's Novgorod and Michael-Voronezh—black.
Nobiliary Regiment—yellow. (The Nobiliary Regiment also had flags from the reign of Emperor Alexander I.)

IRREGULAR FORCES.

The **Don Host** has a St.-George flag with the inscription *"To the loyal Don Host for its services during campaigns: against the Persians in 1826, 1827 and 1828, and against the Turks in 1828 and 1829"*, granted on 23 February 1832 (Illus. 1331a); St.-George flag with the inscription *"For the deeds of the Don Host in the campaign to pacify Hungary and Transylvania 1849"*, granted 26 November 1849.

The **L.-Gds. Cossack Regiment** has St.-George standards with the inscriptions *"For distinction in the defeat and expulsion of the enemy from Russian territory in 1812"* and *"For feats performd at the battle of Leipzig 4 October 1813"*, granted 15 March 1826.

H.I.H. the Heir and Tsesarevich's Leib-Ataman Regiment was ordered to have silver eagles instead of spearheads on the poles of its bunchuk standard and flag, after the pattern for Guards light cavalry, and instead of silver cords and tassels it was to have a St.-George ribbon (16 January and 25 February 1853).

The **Don No. 1 Regiment** has a plain flag with the inscription *"For a distinguished feat during the pacification of Transylvania in 1849"*, granted 19 March 1850 (Illus. 1331b). **Don No. 38 Regiment** has a St.-George flag with the inscription *"For exemplary courage shown during the victory over a mountain tribesmen horde on 3 June 1844 at the Gilli settlement"*, granted 7 May 1845 (Illus. 1332).

The **Black Sea Host** has a St.-George flag with the inscription *"To the loyal host for fifty years of faithful and zealous service marked by brave deeds"*, granted 10 October 1843 (Illus. 1333a).

Black-Sea horse regiments.

No. 1 - 21 September 1831, plain flag with the inscription *"For distinction in the war with Persia and Turkey in 1827, 1828 and 1829"* (Illus. 1333b).

No. 2 - 23 September 1844, plain flag without an inscription (from the 14 flags presented to the Black Sea Host on 10 February 1801).

Nos. 3, 4, 7, 10, 11, and 12 - 23 September 1844, one plain flag each, without inscriptions (from the 6 flags presented to the Host on 31 May 1803).

Nos. 5 and 6 - 23 September 1844, one plain flag each, with the inscription *"For distinction in the Turkish war in 1829"* (Illus. 1333c).

Nos. 8 and 9 - 23 September 1844, one plain flag each with the inscription *"For distinction at the taking of Anapa fortress 12 June 1828"* (Illus. 1334a).

Black-Sea foot battalions.

No. 1 - 23 September 1844, plain flag with the inscription *"For distinction 29 May 1838 at the defeat of the Turkish flotilla at Brailov"* (Illus. 1334b).

Nos. 2, 3, 4, 6, 7, and 9 - 14 March 1845, one plain flag each (Illus. 1334c).

Nos. 5 and 8 - 23 September 1844, with the inscription *"For distinction at the taking of Anapa fortress 12 June 1828"* (Illus. 1334d).

Caucasian Line Cossack Host regiments.

1st Caucasian, 1st and 2nd Laba, 1st and 2nd Stavropol, 1st Khoper, 1st Volga, and Vladikavkaz regiments - 25 June 1851, plain flags with the inscription *"For distinguished and zealous service"* (Illus. 1335a).

2nd Caucasian, 2nd Kuban, 2nd Khoper, 2nd Volga, Mountaineer, Mozdok, and Grebensk regiments - 21 September 1831, plain flags with the inscription *"For distinction in the Turkish war and for battles against the mountain tribesmen in 1828 and 1829"* (Illus. 1335b).

1st and 2nd Kuban regiments - 23 July 1849, with the inscription *"For constant zeal, courage, and dinstinction displayed in all affairs with the mountaineers and especially in the fight of 1 November 1848 at the Sengileevskaya settlement"* (Illus. 1335c).

Kizlyar Regiment - 21 September 1831, two plain flags with the inscription *"For distinction in the Turkish war and for battles against the mountaineers in 1828 and 1829, and for the taking of Andi and Dargo"*. One of these flags was presented to the former Terek Family Cossack Host and the other to he Kizlyar Regiment. The two units later formed the Kizlyar Cossack Regiment.

1st Sunzha Regiment - 6 January 1850, with the inscription "*For distinguished feats during the subjugation of Lesser Chechnya in 1849*".
Caucasian Cossack Foot Battalion - 2 June 1849, plain flag without an inscription.

Azov Host - 1 June 1844, plain host flag, white, with the inscription "*For bravery and zeal during the crossing of the Danube by Russian troops in 1828, constant loyalty, and distinguished service*" (Illus. 1336).
Danube Host, Regiments No. 1 and No. 2 - 15 September 1855, one plain flag each, without an inscription.

Orenburg Host horse regiments.
Nos. 1, 2, 3, 4, 5, 6, 7, 8, 9, and 10 - 18 November 1842, one plain flag each, without inscriptions (Illus. 1337).

Trans-Baikal Host.
Russian Horse Regiments Nos. 1, 2, 3, and 4, and Buryat Horse Regiments Nos. 5 and 6 - 6 December 1852, one plain flag each, without inscriptions.
Foot battalions of the Trans-Baikal Host: Nos. 1, 2, 3, 4, 5, 6, 7, 8, 9, 10, 11, and 12 - 6 December 1852, one plain flag each, without inscriptions.

Caucasian Composite Irregular Regiment - 21 September 1849, plain flag with the inscription "*For distinguished courage displayed in affairs with rebellious Hungarians, and for the battle at Debrecen 21 July 1849*" (Illus. 1338a).
Trans-Caucasus Horse Musulman Regiment - 21 September 1849, St.-George flag with the inscription "*For distinguished courage and bravery in fights against rebellious Hungarians, for the battle of 21 July 1849 at Drebecen, and for taking four guns from the enemy in this affair*" (Illus. 1338b).
Georgian Foot Druzhina - 26 September 1854, plain flag with the inscription "*To our Georgian druzhina for constant distinguished and zealous service in fights with the unsubdued mountaineers*" (Illus. 1339a).
Imeretian Militia - 14 April 1840, red flag with the inscription "*To out Militia of our devoted Imeretian people in reward for distinguished courage displayed against the mountaineers in 1838*" (Illus. 1339b).
Georgian Mass Levy - 7 March 1855, red flag with the inscription "*To the Georgian Mass Levy for constant zeal, devotion, and services as displayed in actions against the mountaineers*" (Illus. 1340a).
Georgian Volunteer Horse Druzhina - 7 March 1855, raspberry St.-George flag with the inscription "*To the Georgian Volunteer Horse Druzhina for its courageous actions during the defeat and pursuit of a Turkish corps beyond the river Cholok 4 June 1851*" (Illus. 1340b).
Samurzakan Mass Levy - 1841, red flag with the inscription "*To the mass levy of our devoted Samurzakan tribe for services performed in 1840 during the introduction of peace in Dale*" (Illus. 1341a).
Inhabitants of Kabarda - 2 March 1844, red flag with the inscription "*To our devoted and loyal Kabardan inhabitants for fidelity and courageous actions against unsubdued mountaineers*" (Illus. 1341b).
Kazikumyk Foot Militia - 15 March 1845, red flag with the inscription "*To the Kazikumyk foot militia for distinction in battles at Kyulyulya-Rugdzha and the Tilitla heights*" (Illus. 1342a).
Kazikumyk Horse Militia - 15 March 1845, red flag with the inscription "*To the Kazikumyk foot militia for distinction in battles at Shaurmko and Rugdzha*" (Illus. 1342b).
Akhta Foot Militia - 15 March 1845, white flag with the inscription "*To the Akhta foot militia for distinction in battles at Dyuvek, Margi, Dokkul-Byar, and the Tilitla heights*" (Illus. 1343a).
Shirvan Horse Militia - 15 March 1845, green flag with the inscription "*To the Shirvan horse militia for distinction in battles at Rugdzha and Dokkul-Byar*" (Illus. 1343b).
Kuban warriors [*Kubinskie voennye nukery*] - 15 March 1845, yellow flag with the inscription "*To the Kuban nuker warriors for distinction in the battles at Kyulyuli Dyuvek and Dokkul-Byar*" (Illus. 1344a).
Kura warriors [*Kurinskie voennye nukery*] - 15 March 1845, dark-blue flag with the inscription "*To the Kura nuker warriors for distinction in the battles at Dyuvek and Pudakar*" (Illus. 1344b).
Inhabitants of Nazran - 31 July 1841, red flag with the inscription "*To our devoted and loyal Nazran inhabitants, for fidelity, bravery, and zeal shown on 7 April 1841*" (Illus. 1345a).
Dzhiget people - 1841, red flag with the inscription "*To the Dzhiget people who in 1841 displayed to us obediance and special devotion*" (Illus. 1345b).

Ossetians of the Vladikavkaz district - 15 March 1845, sky-blue flag with the inscription *"To our devoted and loyal Ossetians of the Vladikavkaz district, for distinguished and zealous service, constant fidelity, and exemplary courage"* (Illus. 1346).

Siberian native peoples.
Buryats of the Khora administration - 20 October 1837, seven red flags and seven sky-blue flags, without inscriptions (Illus. 1347).
Tabanguts of the Batanaevsk, Khochenutsk, and Tabayagutsk tribes - 20 October 1837, three dark-blue flags with the inscription on one of the flags *"To the first Tabangut clan, of the Batanaevsk tribe"*, and on a second *"To the second Tabangut clan, of the Khochenutsk tribe"*, and on the third *"To the third Tabangut clan, of the Tabayagutsk tribe"*.
Buryats of the Oginsk administration (9 clans) - 24 November 1842, nine green flags without inscriptions; Buryats of the Selenginsk administration (15 clans) - 15 August 1845, fifteen of the same flags (Illus. 1348).

Chapter XIX. ORDER RIBBONS AND METAL BANDS FOR FLAGS AND STANDARDS. [*ORDENSKIE LENTY I SKOBY K ZNAMENAM I SHTANDARTAM.*]

25 June 1838 - A HIGHEST Order to the Minister of War laid out:
Wishing to preserve in our victorious army the unforgettable memory of its founder and in each regiment to transmit to the latest descendents its worthy deeds so as to inspire in the most recent generations of brave Russian troops the desire to emulate such glorious battlefield services, we establish three additional special signs of distinction for flags and standards. These distinctions are bestowed according to the following rules:
1. In those regiments and separate units which in one hundred or more years from the time they were first formed have never been disbanded, though they may have changed their name, the infantry on their flags, and the cavalry on their standards, are to have special fringed **order ribbons** according to the confirmed pattern.
2. These ribbons are to be: in the Guards—St. Andrew's, and in the Army and Garrisons—Alexander ribbon.
3. There is to be silver or gold embroidered inscriptions on the ribbons, according to the color of the regiment's buttons: on the front - the year of the regiment's founding and first naming; on the back, for troops having flags and standards with the various inscriptions for distinction or deeds of valor—the year these distinctions were granted.
4. At the end of the ribbon over the fringe are to be stamped metal images: under the year of the regiment's founding—the monogram of the founder; under the year distinctions were granted to the flag or standard—the monogram of the sovereign who granted this distinction. On the opposite end of the reverse side—a two-headed Russian eagle.
5. At the top on a bow, where the ribbon folds over, there is to be a specially embroidered inscription of the year the ribbon was bestowed.
6. Ribbons are to be tied to flags and standards at the upper part of the pole under the eagle or spearhead by a special cord passed through a ring at where the ribbon folds over under the bow.
7. These distinctions are to be considered part of the flag or standard, but used only during regimental holidays, consecrations with holy water, HIGHEST reviews, ceremonial guard mounts for personages of the Imperial family, crowned heads, general-field marshals, and their own honorary colonels, as well as during inspector reviews.
8. Outside these occasions, these ribbons are to be kept in regimental strong boxes under the key and seal of the regimental commander.
9. All regiments and units possessing flags or standards, but not having had 100 years of existence yet, are to have on the pole a gilded bronze round band [*skoba*], slipped on from below over the butt and tightly fastened under the cloth flag or standard.
10. On this metal band is to be: the name of the regiment's founder, the year of founding, the regiment's first name, the distinctions given to the regiment as inscriptions on the flag or standard, the year this distinction was granted, and the name of the regiment and battalion—or double-squadron in the cavalry—to which the flag or standard belongs.
11. These bands are to be for those troops to whom are granted the ribbons established by this order.
When calculating the time since regiments were founded, those regiments that were formed from several units are to count their seniority according to the oldest unit that became part of the regiment, if this unit is no smaller than a half-battalion or two squadrons. However, if a regiment was organized from other regiments through units of a smaller size, then the seniority or formation of the regiment is to be counted from the date it was ordered to be formed.
This order is also effective for flags belonging to cadet corps. They are prescribed St.-Andrew ribbons as in the Guards.

The length of the ribbon established by this order is the same for flags and standards—1 arshin [28 inches], starting from the fold at the top of the pole (Illus. 1349). The width is the same as for the ribbons of the senior grades of knightly orders. Along the ribbon's edges, and across it to separate monograms and eagles from inscriptions, is to be embroidered a gold or silver line, according to the color of the uniform buttons. The cord with which the ribbon is tied to the pole is flat and silver with a mix of black and orange silk (Illus. 1349).

The height of a gilt band fastened by small gilded nails to the pole under the cloth of the flag or standard is 1-1/2 vershoks [2-5/8 inches].

The pattern refered to in the first paragraph and used for all ribbons is the Life-Guards Preobrazhenskii's ribbon, of the sky-blue color particular to the order of St. Andrew the First-Called, and with the followin gold images and inscriptions (Illus. 1349).

On the 1st side—a metallic monogram of Emperor Peter I under an imperial crown, with the embroidered inscription "*1683. The Preobrazhenskii Playthings*", which signified the year the unit that later became the L.-Gds. Preobrazhenskii Regiment was founded, and the title of that unit.

On the 2nd and 3rd sides—the metallic monogram of Emperor Alexander I, who presented the L.-Gds. Preobrazhenskii Regiment with their present flags with their distinctive inscription; the embroidered year the flags were presented—"*1813*", and the inscription itself that is on the flags—"*For distinction in the defeat and expulsion of the enemy from Russian territory in 1812*". At the bottom edge of the 3rd side is a gilded metal image of the two-headed eagle of the Russian imperial coat-of-arms.

On the 4th side—the embroidered inscription "*L.-Gds. Preobrazhenskii Regiment*", i.e. the title of the regiment to which the flag belongs.

On the bow that covers the folding over of the ribbon is the embroidered inscription "*1838*", signifying the year the ribbon was granted.

On the **metal band** are inscribed: the monogram of Emperor Peter I, as founder of the L.-Gds. Preobrazhenskii Regiment, and the inscriptions from all four sides of the ribbon with the addition of the year the ribbon was granted and the number of the battalion to which the flag belongs. For example, in the 1st Battalion after Emperor Peter I's monogram is: "*1683. The Preobrazhenskii Playthings - 1813. For distinction in the defeat and expulsion of the enemy from Russian territory in 1812 - 1838. L.-Gds. Preobrazhenskii Regiment 1st Battalion*" (Illus. 1349).

The **monograms** of sovereigns during whose reigns regiments and other troop units were founded, as well as sovereigns who presented flags with inscriptions to these regiments and units for military distinction, are confirmed in the following styles.

Tsar Michael Feodorovich—of the Old Church Slavonic letters M. F. under the crown of Grand Duke Vladimir Monomach (Illus. 1350a).

Tsar Aleksei Mikhailovich—of the Old Church Slavonic letters A. M. under the same crown (Illus. 1350b).

Emperor Peter I—of Latin letters under an imperial crown (Illus. 1350c).

Empress Catherine I (Illus. 1350d).

Empress Anna Ioannovna (Illus. 1350e).

Empress Elisabeth Petrovna (Illus. 1350f).

Empress Catherine II (Illus. 1350g).

Emperor Paul I (Illus. 1350h).

Emperor Alexander I (Illus. 1350i).

Emperor Nicholas I (Illus. 1350k).

All monograms beginning with that of Emperor Peter I are adopted for ribbons and bands in the style in which they appeared on contemporary flags and standards during each reign. (There were no personal monograms of Emperor Peter II or Emperor Peter III on flags or standards because any regiments or other units founded during their reigns no longer exist.)

Chapter XX. ORDERS AND MEDALS. [ORDENA I MEDALI.]

(This information is taken from Order charters and HIGHEST Orders.)

22 August 1822 - A distinctive insignia is established to mark **irreproachable service**, based on the fact that constant zeal and faultless service over a significant period of time does not have its own authorized distinction other than orders for military officers after 25 years and for civil officials after 35.

This insignia is silver or gilt, and has the form of a rectangular frame buckle on which is depicted a oakleaf wreath; in the center of the wreath in Roman numerals are the number of years of service for which the badge is given, i.e. beginning with 15 years of active service, followed by 20, 25, 30, and so on, for every five years. This mark of distinction for irreproachable service is given to military personnel on a St.-George ribbon, and to civil officials on a St.-Vladimir ribbon (Illus. 1351a and 1351b).

15 March 1828 - All troops who took part in the fighting **against the Persians** in 1826, 1827, and 1828 are ordered to wear a silver medal on a combined St.-George and St.-Vladimir ribbon. On the front of the medal is an eye, and beneath it 1826, 1827, and 1828 in a laurel wreath; on the back is the inscription "*For the Persian War*" (Illus. 1351c).

6 July 1828 - It is ordered that person awarded the order of **St. Anne 3rd class** for military actions are to be distinguished from those who received this order for other services by the addition to the order of a bow of the ribbon prescribed for the order.

April 1828 - A statute for the **order of St. Anne** is confirmed and at the same time it is established that commanders may not put forward recommendations for this order only after the recipient has served in commissioned officer ranks at least 15 years. The statute explains all the rights and privileges of this order, as well as the rules on whose basis various persons may be put forward to be awarded this order.

1 October 1829 - All persons who took part in military operations **against the Turks** in 1828 and 1829 are ordered to wear a silver medal on a St.-George ribbon. On the front of the medal is a cross with two arms and rays of light, standing on a halfmoon with the inscription "*1828 and 1829*" along the cross's sides; on the reverse is the inscription "*For the Turkish War*" within a laurel wreath (Illus. 1351d).

17 November 1831 - It is ordered to join to the orders of the Russian empire the **tsarist Polish orders** of the White Eagle and St. Stanislav, with the designation of these orders as imperial and tsarist [*imperatorskie i tsarskie*].

13 December 1831 - It is ordered that knights of the **order of the apostle St. Andrew the First-Called**, as the most senior order, be also be honored as knights of the order of the White Eagle, with the bestowal of this right to those who in the future may be given the order of St. Andrew in the future, after the date the order of the White Eagle was joined to the system of Russian orders.

31 December 1831 - All persons who took part in **military operations in the Kingdom of Poland** are ordered to wear the badge of distinction for military merit [*znak otlichie za voennye dostoinstva*, i.e. Virtuti Militari - M.C.] that belonged to this kingdom (Illus. 1352a). Those present at the storming of Warsaw are to additionally have a silver medal on whose front is a two-headed eagle over the inscription "*Worth, honor, and glory*", and on the back—a radiant cross over a laurel wreath around the inscription "*For the taking of Warsaw by storm 25 and 26 August 1831*"(Illus. 1352b). The ribbon for the badge of distinction and medal is to be of dark-blue and black stripes.

25 January 1832 - It is ordered to make ribbons for the **order of the White Eagle** in dark blue instead of sky blue (Illus. 1353).

6 December 1833 - A new statute is confirmed for the **Military Order**, in which all previous regulations are joined with certain changes connectd to the order's increased status.

4 February 1835 - It is ordered that persons who received the badge for **irreproachable service** are, in the case of their transfer from military to civilian service and back again, to afterwards be given the badge on the ribbon prescribed for their most recent branch of service.

17 March 1835 - It is ordered that persons holding the orders of the **White Eagle** and **St. Stanislav 1st class** are not to wear either the stars nor the ribbons of these orders with the order of St. Alexander Nevsky (for the first) and with the order of St. Anne 1st class (for the second); to designate the knightly rank of "small cross", with a more senior award they are to wear its cross on the ribbon prescribed for the order.

30 July 1835 - It is ordered that the **Knightly council** consist henceforth of the following numbers of knights: Military order—all 1st and 2nd-class knights present and the 12 senior 3rd and 4th-class knights; St. Vladimir and St. Anne orders—the 12 senior knights of each of these orders' four classes.

10 March 1837 - A new regulation is confirmed for the badge of distinction for **irreproachable service**.

28 May 1839 - As statute is confirmed for the order of **St. Stanislav**, by which only three classes are established instead of the previous four (Illus. 1354).

5 September 1839 - All persons who took part in the **taking of fortified Akhulgo** by storm are ordered to wear a silver medal on St.-George ribbon. On the front of the medal is the Cyrillic monogram N. I, and on the reverse—the inscription "*For the taking of Akhulgo by storm 22 August 1839*" (Illus. 1355a).

4 January 1843 - The following manner for **wearing orders** is established: knights of the order of the apostle St. Andrew the First-Called who wear the cross of the order of St. Alexander Nevsky at the neck on a narrow ribbon are not to wear the insignia of the order of the White Eagle; knights of the order of St. Alexander Nevsky who have the order of the White Eagle and St. Anne 1st class are to wear on the neck only the White Eagle; knights of the order of the White Eagle are to wear at the neck only the order of St. Anne; knights of the order of St. Anne who have the order of St. Stanislav 1st class are to wear it at the neck.

9 August 1844 - It is ordered that all order insignia awarded to **Muslims** replace images of saints with an image of the imperial eagle.

29 August 1844 - A supplementary order was issued that **St.-George medals** awarded to **Muslim lower ranks** also have the image of an imperial eagle.

22 July 1845 - New statutes are confirmed for the orders of **St. Vladimir** and **St. Anne**, along with new guidance for **wearing orders**. Knights of the order of the apostle St. Andrew the First-Called are to wear the order of St. Alexander Nevsky at the neck, but that of the order of the White Eagle—in a buttonhole; knights of the order of St. Alexander Nevsky are to wear the order of the White Eagle at the neck, and that of St. Anne 1st class—in a buttonhole; knights of the order of the White Eagle are to wear the order of St. Anne 1st class at the neck, and that of St. Stanislav 1st class—in a buttonhole; knights of the order of St. Anne 1st class are to wear the order of St. Stanislav 1st class at the neck.

8 January 1846 - It is ordered that henceforth on awarded medals the **visage of His Imperial Majesty** will be with a moustache.

26 February 1846 - It is ordered that order insignia of the first classes which are determined must be worn in a **buttonhole**, are to be arranged not in order of class, but by seniority of the orders, and they are to be of the same size as the insignia of those classes prescribed for wear in buttonholes.

27 October 1846 - On the stars of all orders awarded to **non-Christians**, the images of saints are to be replaced by monograms, and instead of crosses there is to be an imperial eagle.

22 January 1850 - All persons who took part in the **Hungarian war** are ordered to have a silver medal on a combined St. Andrew and St. Vladimir ribbon. On the front of the medal is a two-headed eagle under an all-seeing eye, and around this is the inscription "*God is with us, let it be known and submit*", and on the reverse—the inscription "*For the pacification of Hungary and Transylvania 1849*" (Illus. 1355b).

4 January 1851 - Based on statute, all **St.-George knights** are ordered to also wear the insignia of this order on **frock coats**.

15 July 1854 - It is ordered that all knights of the higher classes of orders be issued **stamped metal stars** instead of the previous embroidered ones.

2 February 1855 - **St.-George knights** who received the order for 25 years of service or 18 campaigns, and who afterwards perform distinguished deeds which confer the right to be awarded the order in 4th class, are ordered to add a bow to the ribbon of the cross they already hold. Along with this it is ordered: 1. Knights awarded the bow are to be titled knights of the military order of St. George 4th class for 25 years service or 18 campaigns with bow; 2. Knights holding the order of St. George 4th class for military deeds are not to be put forward for award of the order for service years or for completing the regulation number of campaigns.

Russian rregular cossacks 1852

NOTES

(163) Complete Collection of the Laws of the Russian Empire, second collection, Vol. VI, sect. 1, No. 4536, pgs. 339, § 14, pg. 340, §§ 18, 20, and 21
(164) Information received from the War Department's Commissariat Department.
(165) Order of the Minister of War, 1838, Book II, pgs. 418-422, and confirmed patterns preserved at the War Department's Commissariat Department.
(166) Order of the Minister of War, 1844, No. 1.
(167) Ditto, 1844, No. 69, pg. 26.
(168) Fifth continuation of the Code of Military Directives, 1845, pgs. 108, 111, and 144-148.
(169) Order of the Minister of War, 1845, No. 66.
(170) Ditto, 1845, No. 72.
(171) Information received from the War Department's Commissariat Department, and confirmed patterns preserved there.
(172) Collection of Laws and Directives, 1837, Book IV, pg. 325.
(173) Ibid., 1838, Book II, pg. 422.
(174) Information received from the War Department's Commissariat Department, and confirmed patterns preserved there.
(175) Order of the Minister of War, 1844, No. 1.
(176) Ditto, 1844, No. 69, pg. 26.
(177) Ditto, 1845, No. 66.
(178) Ditto, 1845, No. 72.
(179) Ditto, 1851, No. 98.
(180) Ditto, 1852, No. 3.
(181) Information received from the War Department's Commissariat Department, and confirmed patterns preserved there.
(182) Ditto.
(183) Collection of Laws and Directives, 1830, Book III, pg. 215.
(184) Information received from the War Department's Commissariat Department.
(185) Collection of Laws and Directives, 1837, Book III, pg. 3.
(186) Ibid., pg. 47.
(187) Ibid., Book IV, pg. 235.
(188) Ibid., 1838, Book II, pgs. 413-422.
(189) Order of the Minister of War, 1844, No. 1.
(190) Ditto, No. 69., pg. 26.
(191) Ditto, 1845, No. 66.
(192) Ditto, No. 72.
(193) Ditto, 1848, No. 16.
(194) Ditto, 1851, No. 6.
(195) Information received from the War Department's Commissariat Department, and confirmed patterns preserved there; information received from the Department of Military Settlements, 8 November 1854, No. 1908.
(196) Collection of Laws and Directives, 1837, Book III, pg. 47.
(197) Ibid., Book IV, pg. 325.
(198) Order of the Minister of War, 1844, No. 1.
(199) Ditto, 1854, No. 134, and HIGHEST confirmed description of patterns, 16 January 1855.
(200) Administrative Regulation for the Government Mobile Mass Levy [*Opolchenie*], confirmed by HIGHEST Authority 29 January 1855.

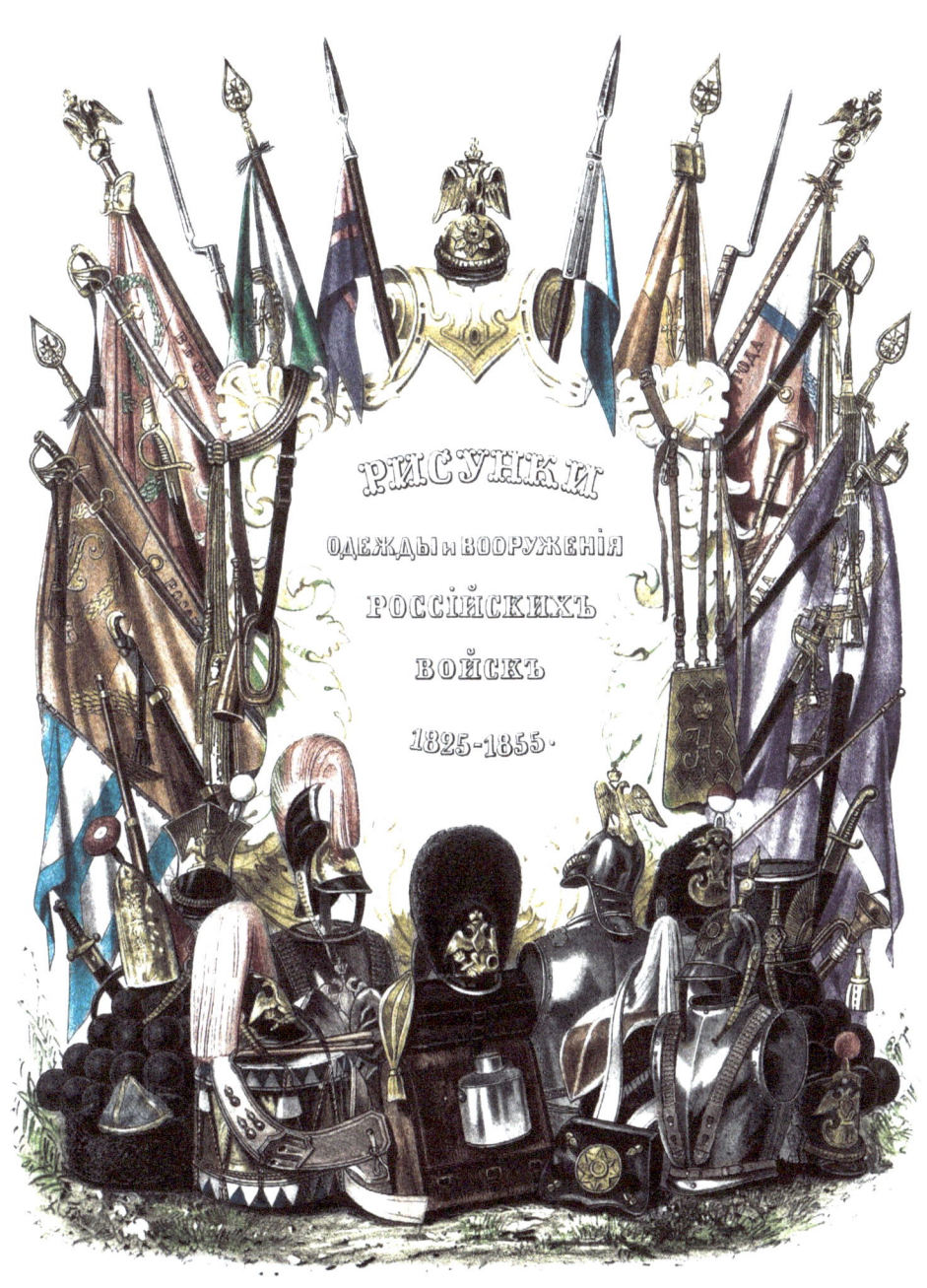

PLATES LIST OF ILLUSTRATIONS

1272. Cossack. Yakutsk Town Cossack Regiment of Foot, 1840-1853.
1273. Noncombatant. Yakutsk Town Cossack Regiment of Foot, 1842-1853.
1274. Cossack, Tobolsk Foot Cossack Battalion, and Field-Grade Officer, Tobolsk Horse Cossack Regiment. 1852-1855.
1275. Field-Grade Officer, Irkutsk Horse Cossack Regiment, and Non-Commissioned Officer, Yeniseisk Horse Cossack Regiment. 1853-1855.
1276. Field-grade Officer and Cossack. Foot Battalions of the Trans-Baikal Cossack Host, 1853-1855.
1277. Cossack. Russian horse regiments of the Trans-Baikal Cossack Host, 1853-1855.
1278. Cossack. Little-Russian Cossack Regiments, 1831-1838.
1279. Company-Grade Officer. Little-Russian Cossack Regiments, 1831-1838.
1280. Non-Commissioned Officer. Little-Russian Cossack Regiments, 1838-1842.
1281. Cossack. Danube Cossack Host. 1837-1838.
1282. Field-Grade Officer. Danube Cossack Host, 1837-1838.
1283. Cossack. Danube Cossack Host. 1844-1845.
1284. Field-Grade Officers. Danube Cossack Host, 1844-1845.
1285. Mounted Cossack. Danube Cossack Host, on internal service, 1844-1845.
1286. Dismounted Cossack. Danube Cossack Host, on internal service, 1844-1855.
1287. Cossack. Danube Cossack Host. 1845-1855.
1288. Company-Grade Officer. Danube Cossack Host. 1845-1855.
1289. Cossack. Azov Cossack Host, 1833-1838.
1290. Company-Grade Officer. Azov Cossack Host, 1833-1838.
1291. Field-Grade Officer. Azov Cossack Host, 1838-1841.
1292. Cossack. Azov Cossack Host, 1841-1845.
1293. Non-Commissioned Officer. Azov Cossack Host, 1841-1845.
1294. Company-Grade Officer. Azov Cossack Host, 1841-1845.
1295. Cossack. Azov Cossack Host, 1845-1855.
1296. Field-Grade Officer. Azov Cossack Host, 1851.
1297. Company-Grade Officer. Azov Cossack Host, 1852-1855.
1298. Private. L.-Gds. Crimean-Tatar Squadron, 1827.
1299. Company-Grade Officer. L.-Gds. Crimean-Tatar Squadron, 1827.
1300. Officer's saddlecloth, L.-Gds. Crimean-Tatar Squadron. *Established 15 July 1827.*
1301. Privates. L.-Gds. Crimean-Tatar Squadron, 1827-1830.
1302. Field-Grade Officer. L.-Gds. Crimean-Tatar Squadron, 1827-1838.
1303. Trumpeter. L.-Gds. Crimean-Tatar Squadron, 1830-1838.
1304. Non-Commissioned Officer. L.-Gds. Crimean-Tatar Squadron, 1838-1845.
1305. Company-Grade Officer. L.-Gds. Crimean-Tatar Squadron, 1838-1845.
1306. Trumpeter. L.-Gds. Crimean-Tatar Squadron, 1845-1855.
1307. Private. L.-Gds. Crimean-Tatar Squadron, 1845-1855.
1308. Field-Grade Officer. L.-Gds. Crimean-Tatar Squadron, 1845-1855.
1309. Company-Grade Officer. L.-Gds. Crimean-Tatar Squadron, 1845-1855.
1310. Private. Balaklava Greek Infantry Battalion, 1830-1855.
1311. Non-Commissioned Officer. Balaklava Greek Infantry Battalion, 1830-1855.
1312. Company-Grade Officer. Balaklava Greek Infantry Battalion, 1830-1855.
1313. Company-Grade Officer and Hornist. Imperial Family Rifle Regiment, 1854-1855.
1314. Rifleman and Non-Commissioned Officer. Imperial FamilyRifle Regiment, 1854-1855.
1315. *Ratnik* and Drummer. Government Mobile Mass Levy [*opolchenie*], 1855.
1316. Non-Commissioned Officer and Company-Grade Officer. Government Mobile Mass Levy, 1855.

1317. Drawings from which the flags for Carabinier regiments were made since 1826.
a) 1st Grenadier Division; b) 2nd Grenadier Division; c) 3rd Grenadier Division and the Erivan Carabinier Regiment; d) Nesvizh Carabinier Regiment.

1318. Drawings from which the flags for Jäger regiments were made since 1826.
a) First Jäger regiments in brigades, except in the Separate Lithuanian Corps; b) First Jäger regiments in brigades in the Separate Lithuanian Corps; c) Second Jäger regiments in brigades, except in the Separate Lithuanian Corps; d) Second Jäger regiments in brigades in the Separate Lithuanian Corps.
Note: The flags in b) and d), until 1831, had a Lithuanian horseman in the eagle's shield.

1319. Drawings of standards, from which flags for Army Cavalry regiments were made since 1826.
a) For all regiments except those in the Lithuanian Lancer Division ; b) For regiments in the Lithuanian Lancer Division.

1320. Drawings from which the flags for Sapper and Pioneer battalions were made:
a) Instructional Sapper Battalion in 1827 ; b) Grenadier Sapper Battalion in 1828 and 1829; c) Pioneer and Sapper battalions, except the Instructional, Grenadier, and Lithuania battalions, since 1828; d) Lithuania Pioneer Battalion in 1828
Note: Up to 1831 the flag in drawing d) had an image of a Lithuanian horseman in the eagle's shield.

1321. Drawing from which the flags Line battalions were made since 1829.

1322. Flags granted to battalions:
a) 2nd Battalion, L.-Gds. Jäger Regiment, in 1828 ; b) L.-Gds. Sapper Battalion in 1828; c) 2nd Battalion, L.-Gds. Lithuania Regiment, in 1832; d) 2nd Battalion, L.-Gds. Volhynia Regiment, in 1832.
Note: In 1830 the spearheads on the flag poles in drawings a) and b) were replaced by the eagles shown in drawings c) and d), but gilded.

1323. Flags granted to battalions:
a) L.-Gds. Finnish Rifle Battalion, in 1829 ; b) the same, in 1831; c) L.-Gds. Garrison Battalion, in 1827.

1324. Standards granted to Guards cavalry units:
a) L.-Gds. Horse Jäger Regiment, in 1827 ; b) L.-Gds. Horse-Pioneer Squadron, in 1826.

1325. Standard granted to the 3rd Double-Squadron [*divizion*] of the L.-Gds. Grodno Hussar Regiment in 1832.

1326. Flag and standard granted to Model regiments in 1836:
a) Infantry ; b) Cavalry.

1327. Flags granted to Instructional Carabinier regiments:
a) 2nd Instructional Carabinier Regiment, 1st and 2nd Battalions in 1832, and 3rd Instructional Carabinier Regiment, the same battalions, in 1837 ; b) 2nd Instructional Carabinier Regiment, 1st and 2nd Battalions; c) 1st Instructional Carabinier Regiment, 1st, 2nd, and 3rd Battalions; d) 4th Instructional Carabinier Regiment, 1st and 2nd Battalions. All the last seven in 1837.

1328. Flags granted to Military Educational institutions:
a) Imperial Military Orphans' Home, in 1826 ; b) Moscow Cadet Corps, in 1827; c) 1st Cadet Corps, in 1832.
Note: in 1830 the spearheads on the flag poles in drawings a) and b) were replaced by eagles of the type shown in drawing c).

1329. Flags granted to Cadet Corps:
a) Graf Arakcheev's Novgorod Cadet Corps, 29 October 1827 ; b) Polotsk Cadet Corps, 29 October 1827; c) Graf Arakcheev's Novgorod Cadet Corps, 9 May 1844.

1330. Flags granted to Cadet Corps:
a) 1st Moscow Cadet Corps, 9 May 1844 ; b) Polotsk Cadet Corps, 9 May 1844; c) Peter-Poltava Cadet Corps, 27 June 1844.

1331. Flags granted to: a) the Don Host in 1832; b) in 1849, and; c) Don No. 1 Regiment in 1850.

1332. Flag granted to Don No. 38 Regiment in 1845.

1333. Flags granted to:
a) Black Sea Cossack Host in 1843 ; b) Black-Sea No. 1 Horse Regiment in 1831; c) Black-Sea Nos. 5 and 6 Horse Regiments in 1844.

1334. Flags granted to:
a) Black-Sea Nos. 8 and 9 Horse Regiments in 1844 ; b) Black-Sea No. 1 Foot Battalion in 1844; c) Black-Sea Nos. 2, 3, 4, 6, 7, and 9 Foot Battalions in 1845; d) Nos. 5 and 8 Battalions in 1844.

1335. Flags granted to:
a) 1st Caucasian, 1st and 2nd Laba, 1st and 2nd Stavropol, 1st Khoper, 1st Volga, and the Vladikavkaz Regiments in 1851

; b) 2nd Caucasian, 2nd Kuban, 2nd Khoper, 2nd Volga, Mountain, Mozdok, Grebentsk, and Kizlyar Regiments in 1831; c) Sunzha Regiment in 1850.

1336. Flag granted to the Azov Cossack Host in 1844.

1337. Flags granted to ten Horse regiments of the Orenburg Cossack Host in 1842.

1338. Flags granted to:
a) Caucasian Composite Irregular Regiment, consisting of Combined Line Cossak-Caucasian Horse-Moutaineer double-squadrons, and b) Trans-Caucasus Horse-Musulman Regiment in 1849.

1339. Flags granted to:
a) Georgian Foot Druzhina in 1854, and b) People of Imeretia in 1839.

1340. Flags granted to:
a) Georgian Mass Levy [*Opolchenie*] in 1842, and b) Georgian Volunteer Horse Druzhinain 1854.

1341. Flags granted to:
a) Samurzakan tribe in 1841, and b) Inhabitants of Kabarda in 1844.

1342. Flags granted to:
a) Kazikumyk Foot Militia and b) Kazikumyk Horse Militia, in 1845.

1343. Flags granted to:
a) Akhta Foot Militia and b) Shirvan Horse Militia in 1845.

1344. Flags granted to:
a) Kuban and b) Kazikumyk warriors [*nukery*] in 1845.

1345. Flags granted to:
a) Nazran inhabitants and b) Dzhiget people in 1845.

1346. Flag granted to the Ossetians of the Vladikavkaz district in 1845.

1347. Flags for the Khora Buryats, seven red and seven sky blue, granted in 1837.

1348. Ten flags granted for the Buryats of the Oginsk administration in 1842 and fifteen for the Buryats of the Selenginsk administration in 1845.

1349. Order ribbon and band for flags of the L.-Gds. Preobrazhenskii Regiment, established 25 June 1838.

1350. HIGHEST personal monograms confirmed for Order ribbons and bands, established 25 June 1838.

1351. Badges for distinction for irreproachable service, since 1827: a) for military officers; b) for civilian officials. Medals for officers and lower ranks: c) for the Persian war of 1826, 1827, and 1828, and d) for the Turkish war of 1828 and 1829.

1352. a) Medal for officers and lower ranks, for the taking of Warsaw by storm in 1831. Crosses for the Polish war: b) for officers and c) for lower ranks.

1353. Imperial and Tsarist order of the White Eagle.

1354. Imperial and Tsarist order of St. Stanislav: a) 1st class, b) 2nd class, and c) 3rd class.

1355. Medals for officers and lower ranks: a) for the taking of Akhulgo by storm, 1839, and b) for the pacification of Hungary and Transylvania in 1849.

1272

Cossack. Yakutsk Town Cossack Regiment of Foot, 1840-1853

1273

Noncombatant. Yakutsk Town Cossack Regiment of Foot, 1842-1853

1274

Cossack, Tobolsk Foot Cossack Battalion, and Field-Grade Officer, Tobolsk Horse Cossack Regiment. 1852-1855

Field-Grade Officer, Irkutsk Horse Cossack Regiment, and Non-Commissioned Officer, Yeniseisk Horse Cossack Regiment. 1853-1855

Field-grade Officer and Cossack. Foot Battalions of the Trans-Baikal Cossack Host, 1853-1855

Cossack. Russian horse regiments of the Trans-Baikal Cossack Host, 1853-1855

1278

Cossack. Little-Russian Cossack Regiments, 1831-1838

1279

Company-Grade Officer. Little-Russian Cossack Regiments, 1831-1838

1280

Non-Commissioned Officer. Little-Russian Cossack Regiments, 1838-1842

1281

Cossack. Danube Cossack Host. 1837-1838

1282

Field-Grade Officer. Danube Cossack Host, 1837-1838

1283

Cossack. Danube Cossack Host. 1844-1845

1284

Field-Grade Officers. Danube Cossack Host, 1844-1845

1285

Mounted Cossack. Danube Cossack Host, on internal service, 1844-1845

1286

Dismounted Cossack. Danube Cossack Host, on internal service, 1844-1855

1287

Cossack. Danube Cossack Host. 1845-1855

1288

Company-Grade Officer. Danube Cossack Host. 1845-1855

1289

Cossack. Azov Cossack Host, 1833-1838

1290

Company-Grade Officer. Azov Cossack Host, 1833-1838

1291

Field-Grade Officer. Azov Cossack Host, 1838-1841

1292

Cossack. Azov Cossack Host, 1841-1845

1293

Non-Commissioned Officer. Azov Cossack Host, 1841-1845

1294

Company-Grade Officer. Azov Cossack Host, 1841-1845

1295

Cossack. Azov Cossack Host, 1845-1855

1296

Field-Grade Officer. Azov Cossack Host, 1851

1297

Company-Grade Officer. Azov Cossack Host, 1852-1855

1298

Private. L.-Gds. Crimean-Tatar Squadron, 1827

1299

Company-Grade Officer. L.-Gds. Crimean-Tatar Squadron, 1827

1301

Privates. L.-Gds. Crimean-Tatar Squadron, 1827-1830

1302

Field-Grade Officer. L.-Gds. Crimean-Tatar Squadron, 1827-1838

1303

Trumpeter. L.-Gds. Crimean-Tatar Squadron, 1830-1838

Non-Commissioned Officer. L.-Gds. Crimean-Tatar Squadron, 1838-1845

1305

Company-Grade Officer. L.-Gds. Crimean-Tatar Squadron, 1838-1845

1306

Trumpeter. L.-Gds. Crimean-Tatar Squadron, 1845-1855

1307

Private. L.-Gds. Crimean-Tatar Squadron, 1845-1855

1308

Field-Grade Officer. L.-Gds. Crimean-Tatar Squadron, 1845-1855

Company-Grade Officer. L.-Gds. Crimean-Tatar Squadron, 1845-1855

1310

Private. Balaklava Greek Infantry Battalion, 1830-1855

Non-Commissioned Officer. Balaklava Greek Infantry Battalion, 1830-1855

1312

Company-Grade Officer. Balaklava Greek Infantry Battalion, 1830-1855

1313

Company-Grade Officer and Hornist. Imperial Family Rifle Regiment, 1854-1855

Rifleman and Non-Commissioned Officer. Imperial Family Rifle Regiment, 1854-1855

1315

Ratnik and Drummer. Government Mobile Mass Levy [opolchenie], 1855.

1316

Non-Commissioned Officer and Company-Grade Officer. Government Mobile Mass Levy, 1855

1300 - 1350

Officer's saddlecloth, L.-Gds. Crimean-Tatar Squadron. Established 15 July 1827
HIGHEST personal monograms confirmed for Order ribbons and bands, established 25 June 1838

1317 - 1318

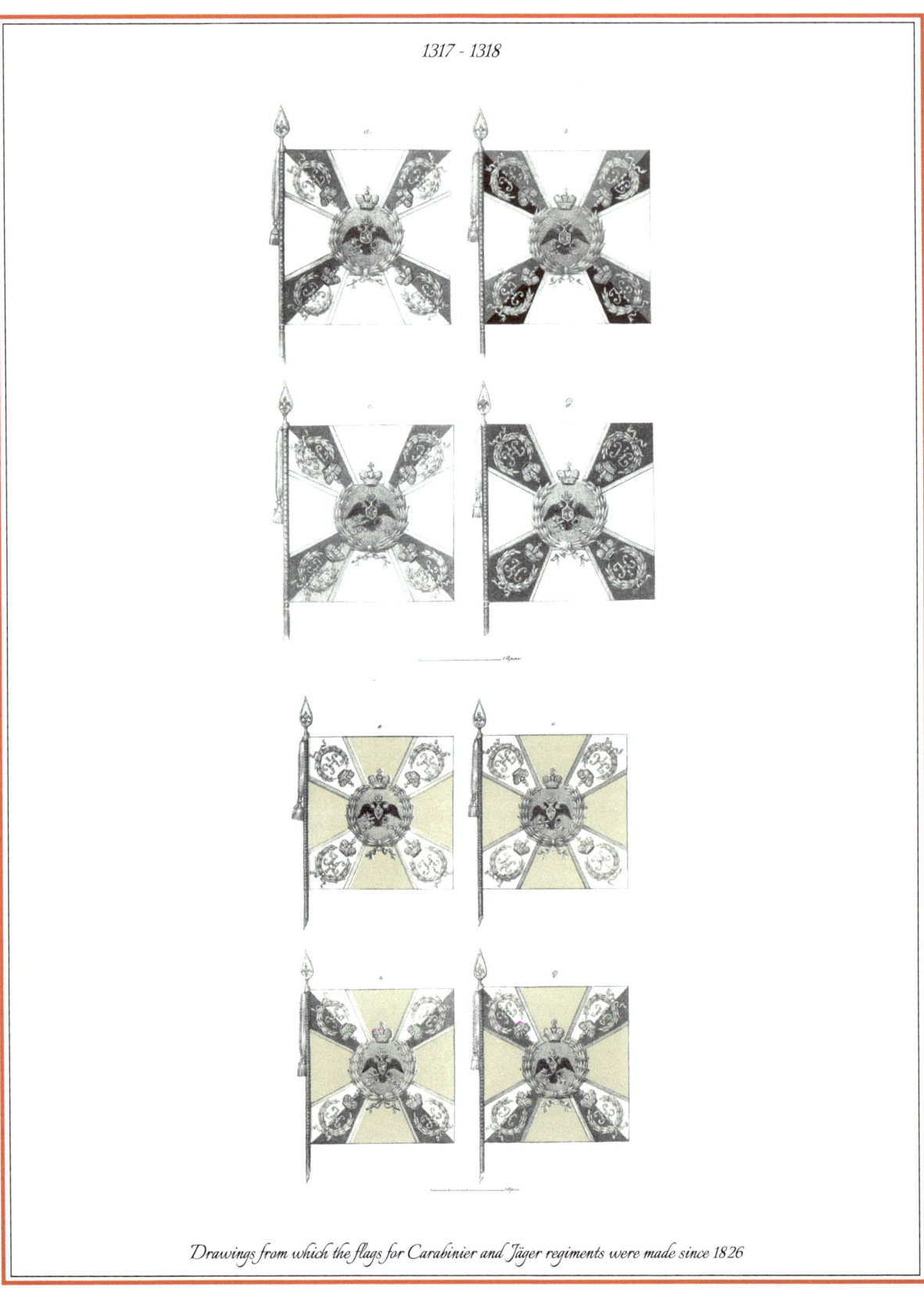

Drawings from which the flags for Carabinier and Jäger regiments were made since 1826

1319 - 1324

Drawings of standards, from which flags for Army Cavalry regiments were made since 1826
Standards granted to Guards cavalry units

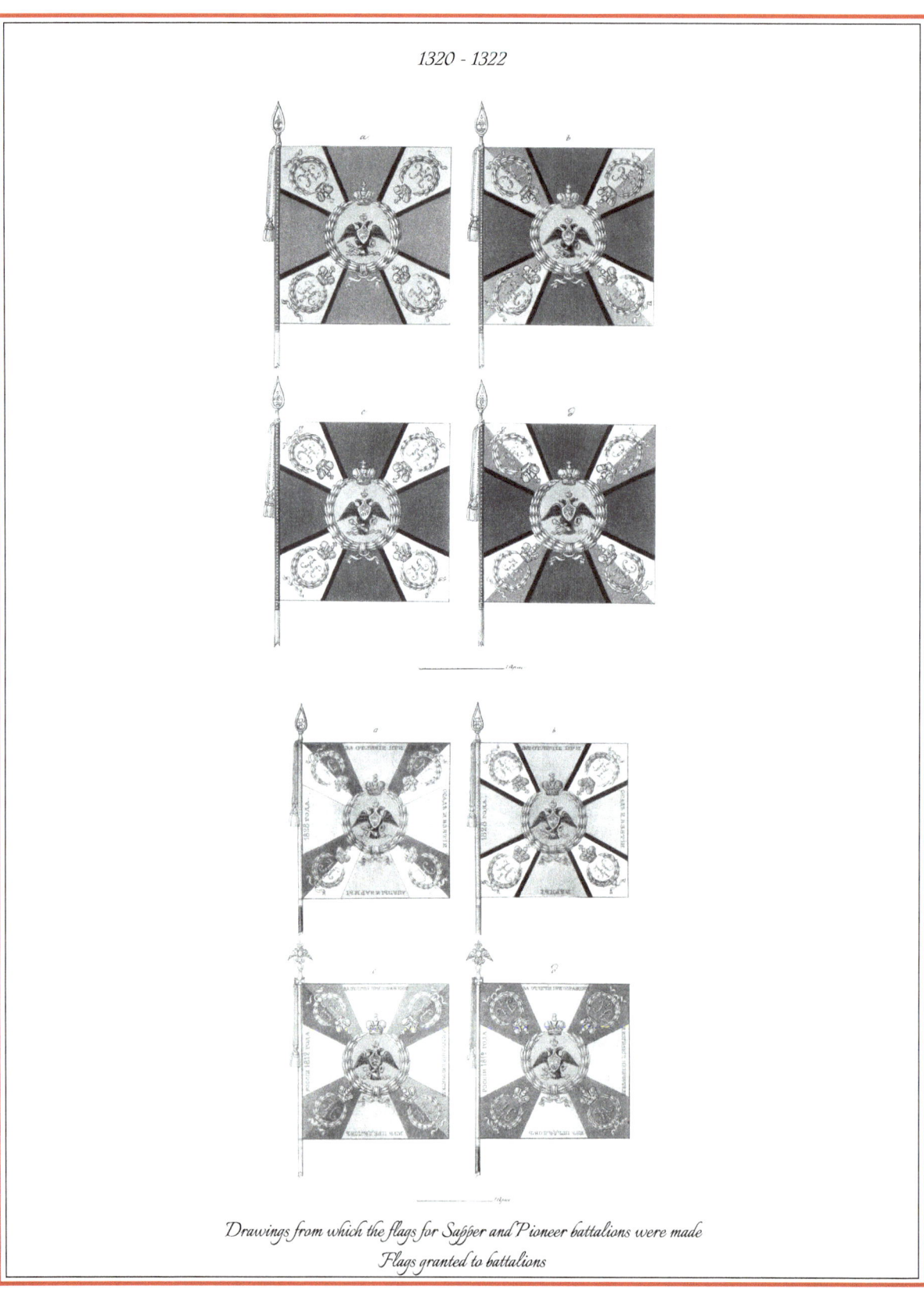

Drawings from which the flags for Sapper and Pioneer battalions were made
Flags granted to battalions

1321 - 1325

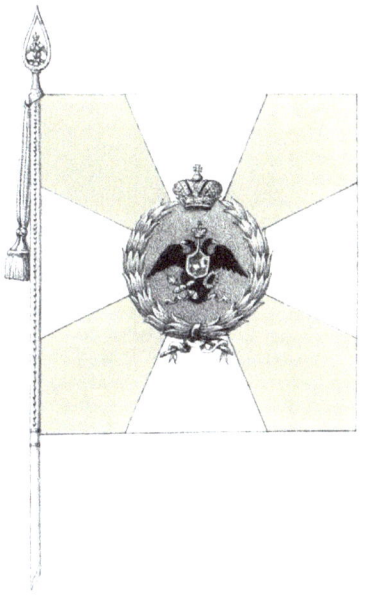

Drawing from which the flags Line battalions were made since 1829
Standard granted to the 3rd Double-Squadron [divizion] of the L.-Gds. Grodno Hussar Regiment in 1832

1327 - 1331

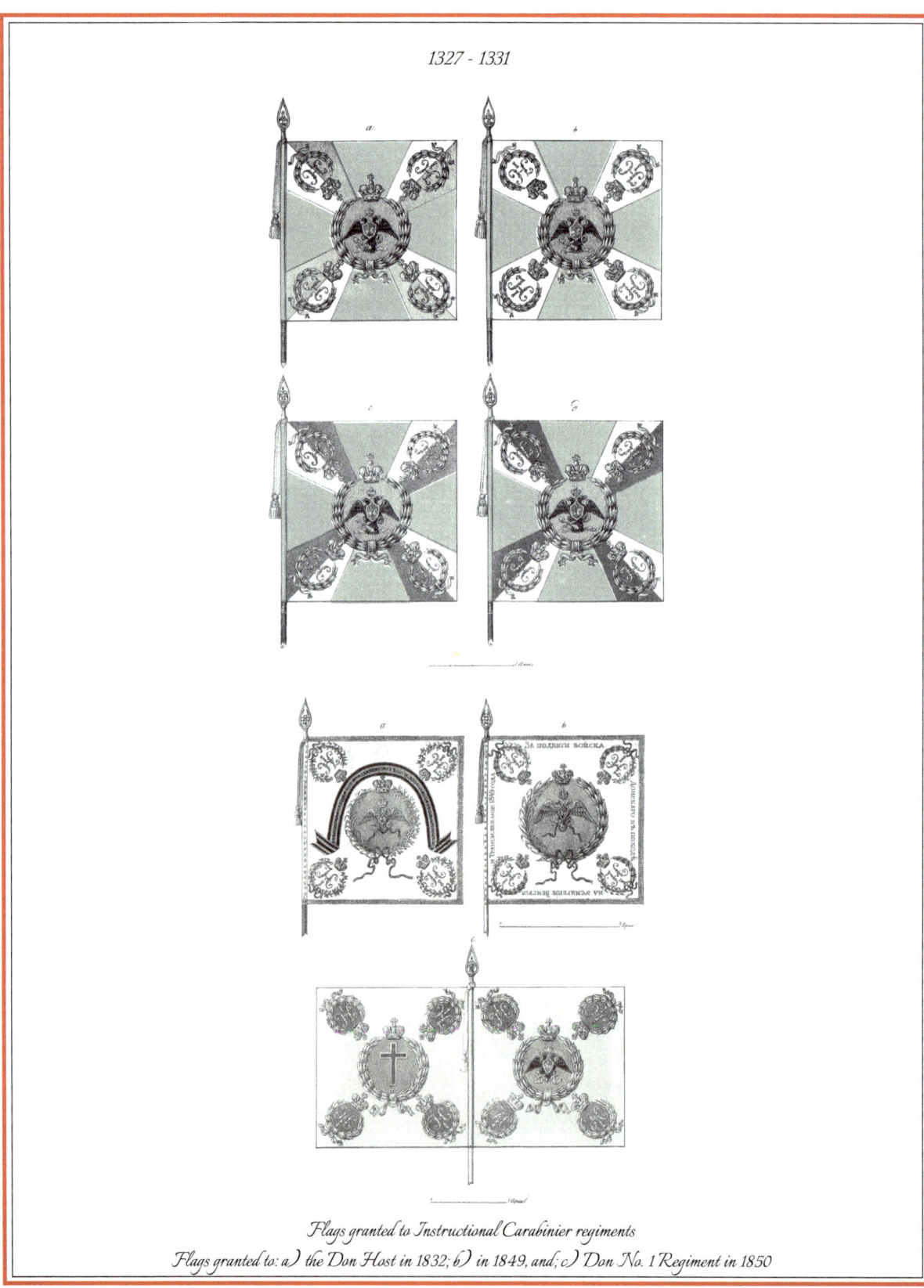

Flags granted to Instructional Carabinier regiments
Flags granted to: a) the Don Host in 1832; b) in 1849, and; c) Don No. 1 Regiment in 1850

1328 - 1329

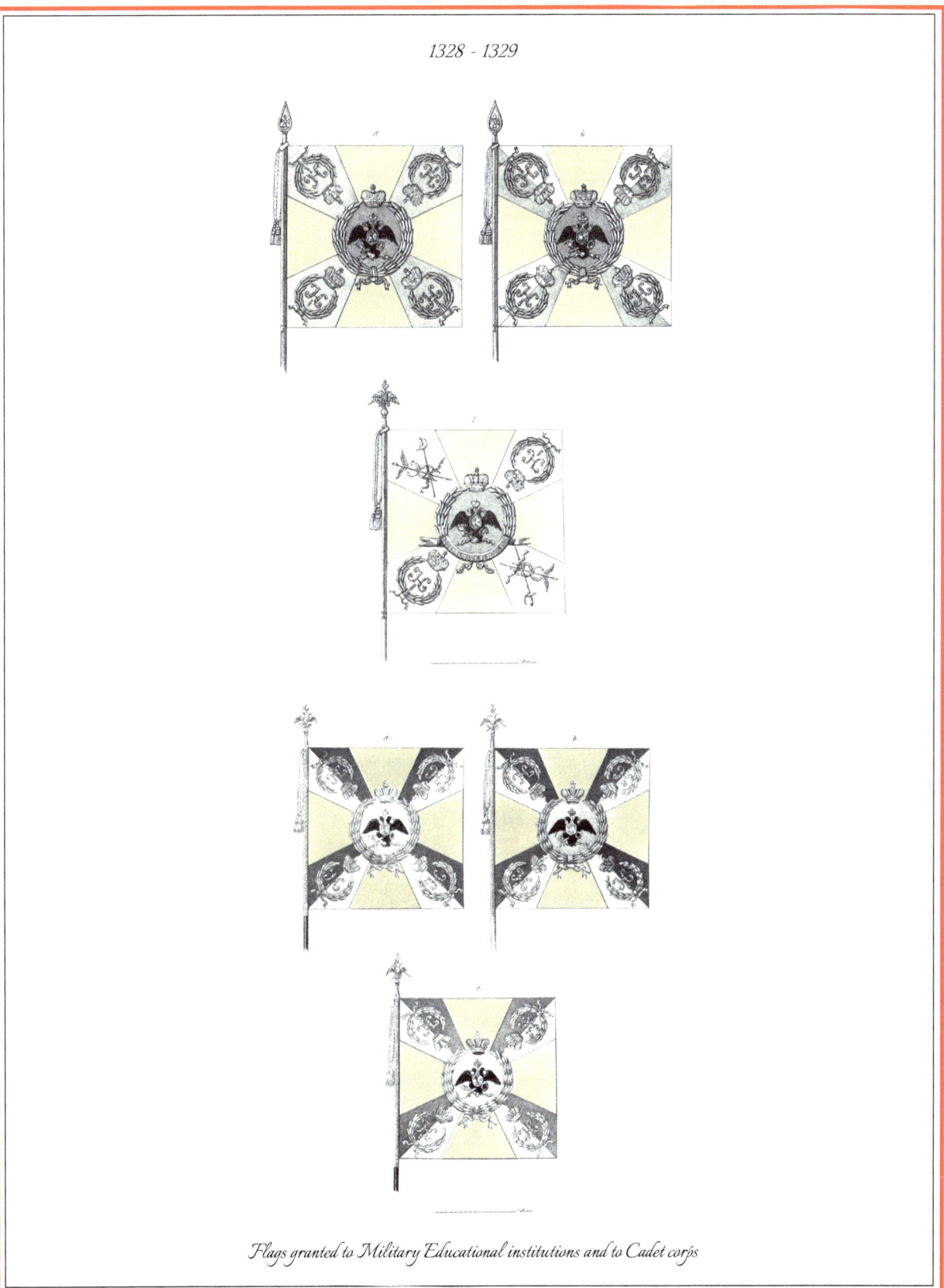

Flags granted to Military Educational institutions and to Cadet corps

1330 - 1332

Flags granted to Cadet Corps and Don no. 38 Regiment in 1845

1333 - 1334

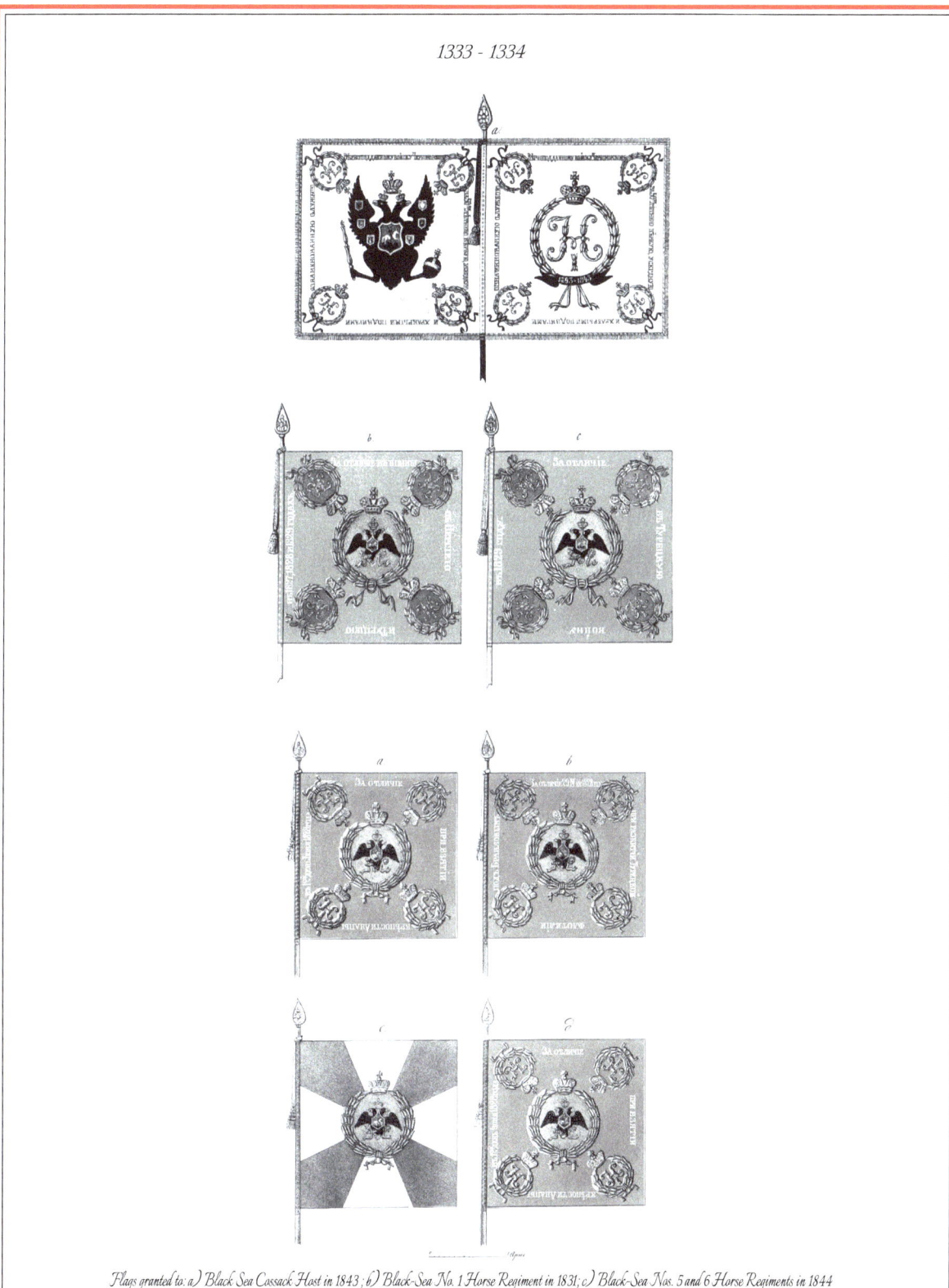

Flags granted to: a) Black Sea Cossack Host in 1843; b) Black-Sea No. 1 Horse Regiment in 1831; c) Black-Sea Nos. 5 and 6 Horse Regiments in 1844

Flags granted to: a) Black-Sea No. 8 and 9 Horse Regiments in 1844; b) Black-Sea No. 1 Foot Battalion in 1844; c) Black-Sea No. 9 Foot Battalions in 1845; d) No. 5 and 8 Battalions in 1844

1335 - 1338

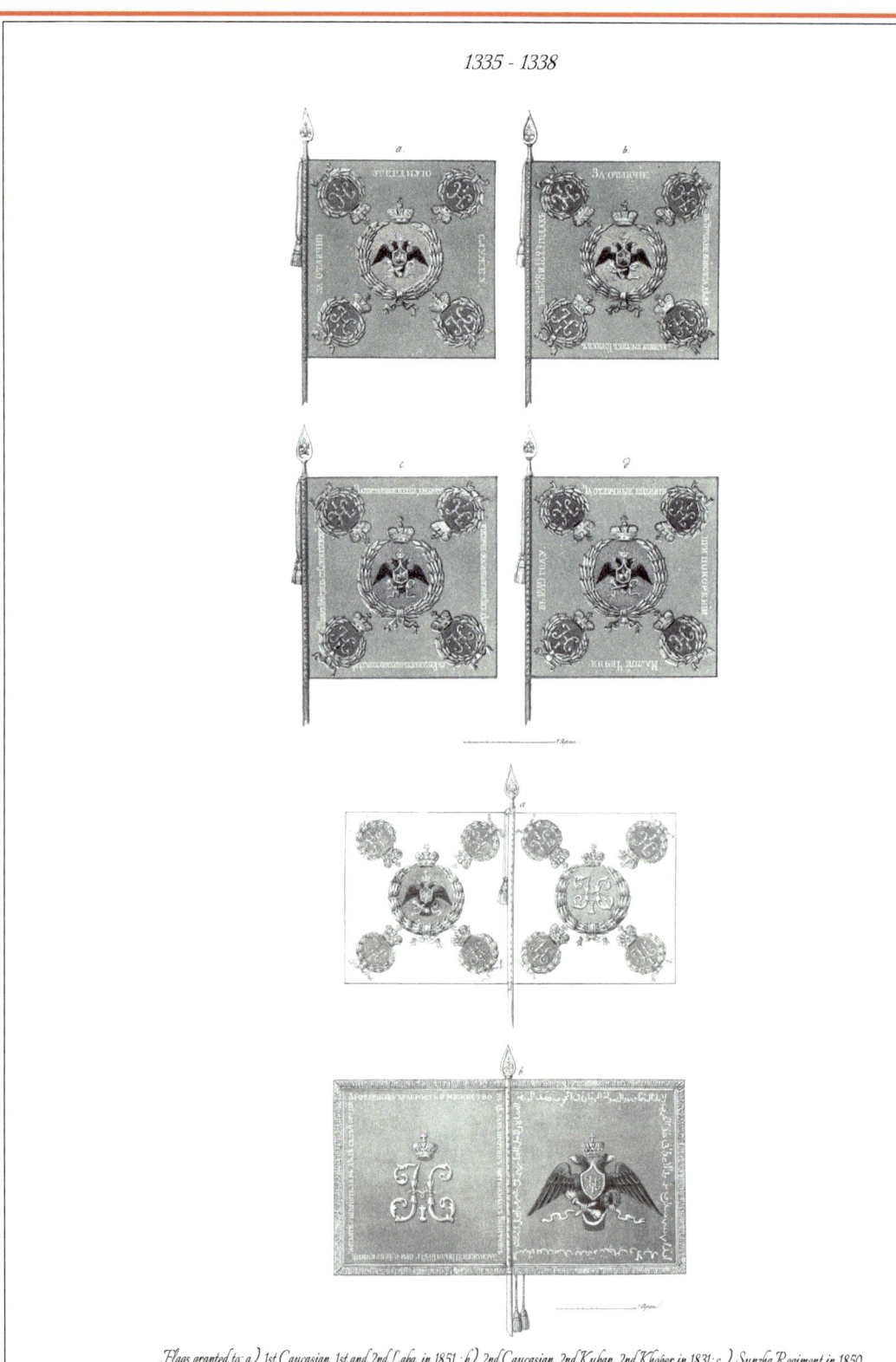

Flags granted to: a) 1st Caucasian, 1st and 2nd Laba, in 1851; b) 2nd Caucasian, 2nd Kuban, 2nd Khoper in 1831; c) Sunzha Regiment in 1850

Flags granted to: a) Caucasian Composite Irregular Regiment, and b) Trans-Caucasus Horse-Musulman Regiment in 1849

Flag granted to the Azov Cossack Host in 1844
Flags granted to ten Horse regiments of the Orenburg Cossack Host in 1842

1339 - 1340

Flags granted to: a) Georgian Foot Druzhina in 1854, and b) People of Imeretia in 1839
Flags granted to: a) Georgian Mass Levy [Opolchenie] in 1842, and b) Georgian Volunteer Horse Druzhina in 1854

1341 - 1342

Flags granted to: a) Samurzakan tribe in 1841, and b) Inhabitants of Kabarda in 1844
Flags granted to: a) Kazikumyk Foot Militia and b) Kazikumyk Horse Militia, in 1845

1343 - 1344

Flags granted to: a) Akhta Foot Militia and b) Shirvan Horse Militia in 1845

Flags granted to: a) Kuban and b) Kazikumyk warriors [nukery] in 1845

1345 - 1347

Flags granted to: a) Nazran inhabitants and b) Dzhiget people in 1845
Flags for the Khora Buryats, seven red and seven sky blue, granted in 1837

1346 - 1348

Flag granted to the Ossetians of the Vladikavkaz district in 1845

Ten flags granted for the Buryats of the Oginsk administration in 1842 and fifteen for the Buryats of the Selenginsk administration in 1845

1349 - 1355

Order ribbon and band for flags of the L.-Gds. Preobrazhenskii Regiment, established 25 June 1838
Medals for officers and lower ranks: a) for the taking of Akhulgo by storm, 1839, and b) for the pacification of Hungary and Transylvania in 1849

1351 - 1352

Badges for distinction for irreproachable service, since 1827: a) for military officers; b) for civilian officials. Medals for officers and lower ranks: c) for the Persian war of 1826, 1827, and 1828, and d) for the Turkish war of 1828 and 1829 - a) Medal for officers and lower ranks, for the taking of Warsaw by storm in 1831. Crosses for the Polish war: b) for officers and c) for lower ranks

Imperial and Tsarist order of the White Eagle
Imperial and Tsarist order of St. Stanislav: a) 1st class, b) 2nd class, and c) 3rd class

SOLDIERS, WEAPONS & UNIFORMS ALREADY PUBLISHED
(SOME TITLES)

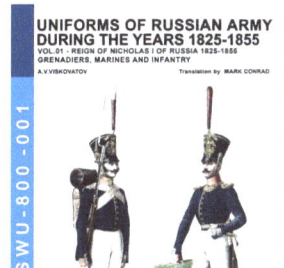
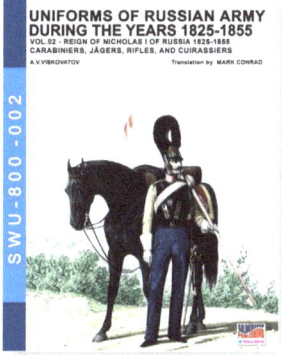
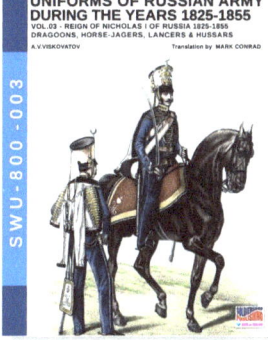
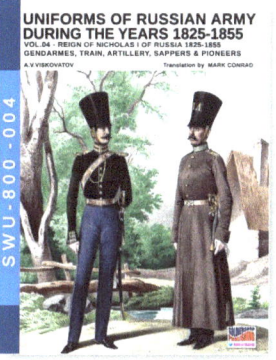

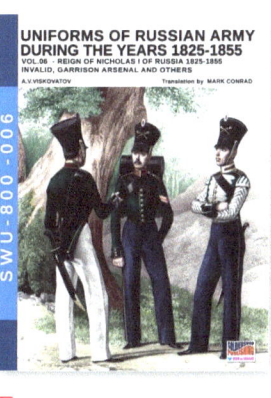
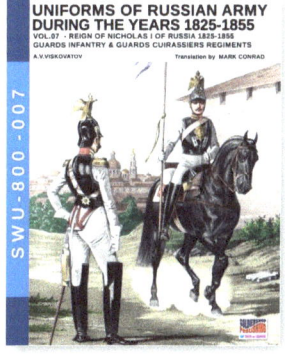
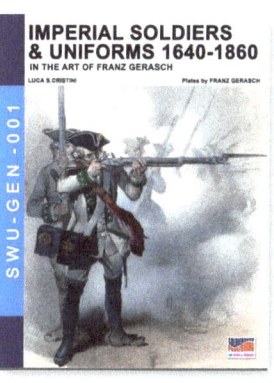
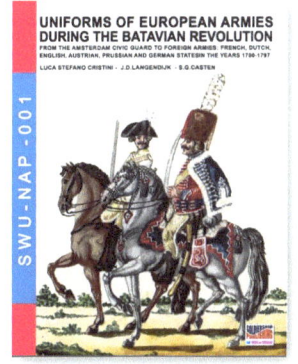

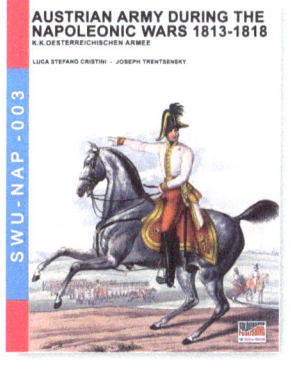
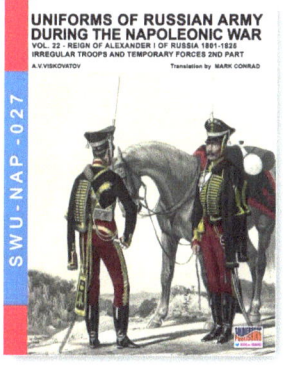
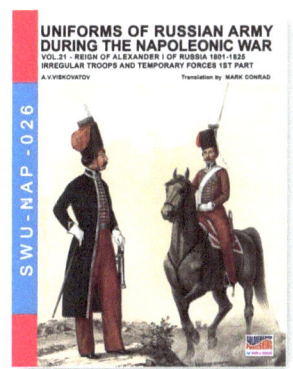
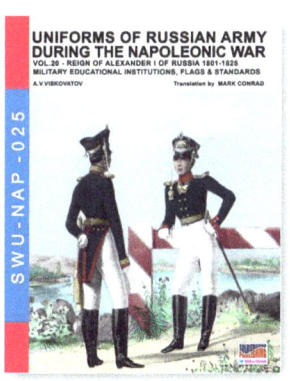
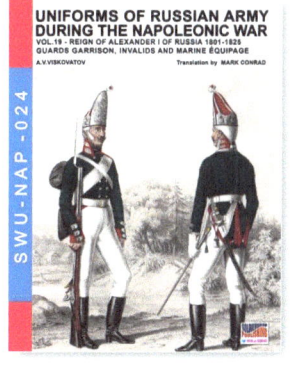
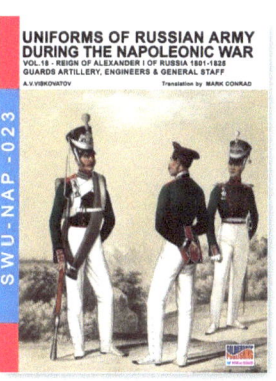

www.ingramcontent.com/pod-product-compliance
Lightning Source LLC
Chambersburg PA
CBHW041121300426
44112CB00003B/49